MW00535078

THE COMPLETE GUIDE TO RAISING AND EMPOWERING AN ADHD CHILD

Download the Audio Book Version of This Book for FREE

If you love listening to audio books on-the-go, I have great news for you. You can download the audio book version of this book for **FREE** just by signing up for a **FREE** 30-day Audible trial! See below for more details!

As an audible customer, you will receive the below benefits with your 30-day free trial:

- FREE audible book copy of this book
- After the trial, you will get 1 credit each month to use on any audiobook
- Your credits automatically roll over to the next month if you don't use them
- Choose from Audible's 200,000 + titles
- Listen anywhere with the Audible app across multiple devices
- Make easy, no-hassle exchanges of any audiobook you don't love
- Keep your audiobooks forever, even if you cancel your membership

Click the links below to get started!

For Audible US

https://www.audible.com/pd/B09NNS88XD/?source_code=AUDFPWS0223189MWT-BK-ACX0-290151&ref=acx_bty_BK_ACX0_290151_rh_us

For Audible UK

https://www.audible.co.uk/pd/B09NNR39Z9/?source_code=AUKFrDlWS02231890H6-BK-ACX0-290151&ref=acx_bty_BK_ACX0_290151_rh_uk

For Audible FR:

https://www.audible.fr/pd/B09NNSXS58/?source_code=FRAORWS022318903B-BK-ACX0-290151&ref=acx_bty_BK_ACX0_290151_rh_fr

For Audible DE

https://www.audible.de/pd/B09NNSSQ1T/?source_code=EKAORWS0223189009-BK-ACX0-290151&ref=acx_bty_BK_ACX0_290151_rh_de

Thank you for purchasing my book. I have 2 GIFTS FOR YOU: MY audiobook and a free video course regarding "How To Discipline Your Child with ADHD". You can download these materials for free from this link: https://dl.bookfunnel.com/b8yw5x4m7t

Table of Contents

V

X

INTRODUCTION

ADHD is Attention Deficit Hyperactivity Disorder (or ADD) and is a neurological disorder that affects the brain's concentration and attentional capacities.It is a common condition that can affect the general performance of a child, whether at home or school, and even friendship. Impulsivity and hyperactivity are signs and symptoms of ADHD, which are both related to brain activity.

ADHD is a condition where it's difficult for people to concentrate or sit still for an extended period of time. Both children and adults can have ADHD, and like most neurological disorders, the signs and symptoms can be seen in almost every individual. The frequency of occurrence of these signs and symptoms is what tells whether a person has ADHD or not.

It is completely normal for a person to think of different things at a time. Sometimes when watching a movie or talking to someone, you'll realize that you are thinking of something completely unrelated to what you are watching. That does not mean that you have ADHD because you can always channel your thoughts back to what you were previously doing, and focusing is a lot easier for you.

In patients with ADHD, it's a lot harder for them to maintain focus, which is why it greatly affects their quality of life. Paying attention to what the teacher is saying at school or when they do their homework is difficult for kids. It is totally normal for a child to forget their homework or even have a daydream in class. Sometimes kids act irrationally or get fidgety. As parents, you need to understand the nature of ADHD and the importance of employing effective strategies towards managing the condition.

Impulsivity, hyperactivity, and inattention are the general signs of ADHD, and it is worth mentioning that ADHD is sometimes referred to as ADD. Differentiating between a normal kid's behavior and ADHD can be tricky because identifying only a few signs and symptoms doesn't outrightly mean that your child has ADHD. Also, living with a child that has ADHD can be overwhelming and frustrating. However, as a parent, you need to be aware of all the things you can do to overcome daily challenges and also to help in controlling the symptoms.

To help you understand what ADHD is, here are some myths and facts about the disorder:

Myth: Every child with ADHD is hyperactive

Fact: Not all kids with ADHD will show hyperactivity symptoms. In most cases, the main problem is with attention, and these types of children will always appear unmotivated and rather boring.

Myth: Every child with ADHD will find it hard to pay attention

Fact: It is totally normal for kids with ADHD to concentrate on different activities. However, maintaining focus, especially

if the task is repetitive or boring, becomes the major issue for
such kids.

Myth: Kids with ADHD can decide to behave better

Fact: No matter how hard a child with ADHD tries to focus
or concentrate on an activity, they still find it difficult to stay
quiet, still, or even pay attention. Sometimes, these kids may
appear disobedient and stubborn, but it doesn't mean that they
are doing it on purpose.

Myth: Kids will eventually outgrow ADHD

Fact: In most cases, ADHD will continue into adulthood
which is why you should act fast rather than wait for the child
to outgrow it. Treatment is generally effective and can help
bring the symptoms to the barest minimum.

**Myth: Medication is the most effective and best treatment
for ADHD**

Fact: Even though they are often prescribed as first-line
treatment for ADHD, it is not always the best remedy for the
condition. There are so many other effective treatments for
ADHD, and this includes behavior therapy, proper nutrition,
exercise, and support in school or at home.

1 ADHD AND ADHD TREATMENT

1.1 What is ADHD?

1.1.1 How ADHD Affects Kids

ADHD may make children energetic, impulsive, and distractible more than their ordinary age. Young children with ADHD find it difficult to develop new skills, including controlling their behavior, maintaining attention, expend energy, and regulate their emotions. This is the main reason why it is often hard for parents to manage kids with ADHD.

Here are some reasons why managing kids with ADHD may be a lot harder:

- **Such kids are distractible:** Kids with ADHD are distractible and often have trouble paying attention, show poor effort in schoolwork, need many reminders to do things, do not follow directions well, and are unable to listen well.

- **Such kids are hyperactive:** Kids with ADHD are usually disorganized and messy. Sometimes they fidget frequently and are unable to sit still. If you have a kid with ADHD, you'll notice that they usually make careless mistakes, mostly because they rush frequently and cannot take their time to do things. You'll find such kids climbing or jumping unnecessarily.

- **Such kids are impulsive:** A child with ADHD may do things irrationally and mostly do what they are not supposed to do. Sometimes these kids will lose their temper or have an emotional outburst.

Parents will first believe these actions are perfectly typical with their children and merely seem to have misbehaved the youngster. Parents may be distracted, irritated, and stressed by ADHD.

You might feel rather embarrassed with your child's behavior or wonder if you are responsible for their behavior. For kids with ADHD, they don't naturally have the skills that control behavior, activity, and attention.

Parents will learn best from ADHD and the best methods to deal with the issue and improve their child's quality of life.

1.1.2   Brief History of ADHD

As far back as 1798, a Scottish doctor named Alexander Crichton observed the easy distractibility of some people. He also observed that some people were unable to focus on activities easily. This prompted him to research deeper into the possible causes, and soon he realized that these symptoms were present even in early life, which is consistent with what is now referred to as ADHD.

In 1902, Sir George Frederic, in many lectures, talked about a mental condition that was present even in completely normal, healthy, and intelligent children. These kids were impulsive, with problems associated with self-control and attention. Sir George also carried out his research using different kids, in which he noted five cases in young girls and 15 in boys. Further research also shows that males are generally more likely to have ADHD than females, and this information has been confirmed by many research works.

Hyperkinetic illness was first discovered by German physicians Hans Pollnow and Franz Kramer in 1932. It was very difficult for kids with this condition to stay still, and following rules, even in classes or other activities, was a lot harder for such kids. The condition was identified in kids as young as 3 years. However, further research proved that these kids could outgrow this condition, and as soon as they clocked 7 years, their restlessness reduced significantly. Some even got better with age.

Charles Bradley, in 1937 first noticed that Benzedrine, a stimulant, helped children to behave better. He also observed that the performance of these kids improved significantly. Benzedrine was first approved by the FDA in 1936, but it took a year before Bradley made his findings of its effectiveness in managing ADHD.

Several other drugs have been used in managing ADHD, but today, methylphenidate is the main stimulant that's used by doctors in different parts of the world. This drug was discovered in 1944, and in 1954, it was marketed as Ritalin. Initially, it was shown to help treat symptoms of ADHD.

The original DSM (diagnostic and statistical manual) did not include ADHD, a significant gap in the system. Attention deficit hyperactivity disorder (ADHD) was initially listed in the second edition of the Diagnostic and Statistical Manual (DSM-II) in 1968. However, the condition was referred to as a hyperkinetic reaction of childhood. In 1980, APA changed the name to attention deficit disorder, and two variations were created: ADHD without hyperactivity and ADHD with hyperactivity. In 1987, the symptoms of hyperactivity, impulsivity, and inattentiveness were all bundled together to create the term attention deficit hyperactivity disorder (ADHD).

1.1.3   Data and Statistics for ADHD

A study published in the Lancet estimates that as many as 3.4 million U.S. and internationally enrolled youngsters may have been diagnosed with ADHD. Approximately 6 million American children have been diagnosed with ADHD, according to a recent national survey of parents. This number accounts for

- a total of 2.4 million youngsters aged 6 to 11
- 388,000 children within age 2 to 5 years
- 3.3 million children within the age 12 to 17 years

The survey also revealed that male children are at higher risk of ADHD compared to female children. One thing to note is that the number of children diagnosed with ADHD is always on the increase. It was around 4.5 million in 2003 but has steadily increased over the past few years, and in 2016, it rose to 6.1 million children.

Other problems have also been found to be more prevalent in children with ADHD. According to the study, almost six out of every ten (6/10) children diagnosed with ADHD also had another mental, behavioral, or emotional problem.

- 3/10 children diagnosed with ADHD had anxiety
- 5/10 children diagnosed with ADHD had conduct or behavioral problem

Other conditions often associated with ADHD include autism spectrum disorder, Tourette syndrome, and depression.

The 2016 parent survey extends further to the treatment strategies used for children diagnosed with ADHD. 3/4 children with ADHD have received one form of treatment or the other.

- Of those 65% of kids who were treated, 18% were prescribed ADHD medication between 2 to 5 years, 69% were prescribed ADHD medication within 6 to 11 years, and 62% were prescribed ADHD medication within 12 to 17 years.
- About 47% of kids with ADHD have received behavioral treatment, of which 60 of kids within 2 to 5 years, 51% of kids within 6 to 11 years, and 42% of kids within 12 to 17 years have received behavioral treatment.
- In general, about 80% of these children have received one form of treatment or the other. Also, 30% have been treated using medications alone, 15% with behavioral treatment alone, and 32% with both treatment strategies.
- About 25% of treated kids were treated with neither behavioral treatment nor the use of medication. It remains unclear the type of treatment received by these children.

A vast majority of the children diagnosed with ADHD have received some type of service in the past. Surveys have also been carried out by parents of children, especially those who have been diagnosed with ADHD and are within 4 to 17 years. The data from this survey is as follows:

- 9/10 children diagnosed with ADHD in addition to educational assistance, students have gotten support for their studies
- 6/10 children diagnosed with ADHD have received skills training and other behavioral treatment. This term's other treatments include peer counseling, social skills training, cognitive behavioral therapy, and parent counseling.

There are so many healthcare claims in addition to the parent-reported data. One of such healthcare claims suggested the following:
- Within 2008 and 2011, one of such healthcare data suggested that children of ages 2 to 5 were likely to get clinical care for ADHD
- 3 out of 4 children who have received clinical care for ADHD also received medication and other psychological services

The exact psychological services that these kids received remains unknown; it's certain that they received psychological treatment.

1.2   Causes of ADHD and Risk Factors

Most of the available research into the causes of ADHD links the condition with hereditary and genetic causes. Scientists continue to investigate whether genes are the sole factors responsible for causing ADHD. The genes in question are mainly those that are linked to dopamine. Dopamine is a neurotransmitter that is known to have a crucial impact in the ADHD diagnosis. Other professionals are of the opinion that our consumer-driven, stressed-out, and fast-paced lives can also trigger ADHD

The exact cause of ADHD remains unknown. There are so many factors that can be attributed to cause ADHD. this includes nutrition, genetics, and problems with the central nervous system, among other factors

1.2.1   Genes and ADHD

There's enough evidence to show that ADHD is influenced by many genetic factors. It has been proven to run in many families and can also affect close relatives. This means that a parent with ADHD will most like have a parent or both parents with ADHD. It is still unknown the exact gene responsible for ADHD, but there's sufficient evidence to show that genes influence ADHD.

The exact gene responsible for ADHD remains unknown, but there are so many connections between DRD4 genes and ADHD. Research also shows that these genes can affect dopamine receptors in the brain, and people with ADHD often have these genes in different variations. This remains the main reason why many believe that genes have a role to play in developing ADHD. Also, there is more than one gene that has been linked with ADHD.

Today, part of the diagnostic methods used in identifying ADHD in individuals involve analyzing the family history of affected people. The environment, in addition to several other factors, can also influence the development of the disorder.

1.2.2   Neurotoxins and ADHD

Researchers also believe that there are many neurotoxic chemicals that are involved in the development of ADHD. Examples of this include pesticides and lead. Lead is a toxic compound, and it is usually advised that both adults and kids should avoid exposure to this compound. When kids are exposed to Lead, it may affect and alter their performance, as well as the level of education they achieve. Lead exposure is also associated with hyperactivity, impulsivity, and inattention.

Organophosphate pesticides are also associated with ADHD. These chemicals are usually used on lawns and even on some agricultural products. One thing you must note about the use of organophosphates is that they are toxic and can pose serious adverse events on the neurodevelopment of children.

1.2.3   Nutrition and ADHD

Even though there are no concrete evidence to suggest this, many believe that preservatives and food dyes can influence ADHD, particularly hyperactivity in children. Foods with artificial agents like coloring and even snacky foods are usually thought to make kids hyperactive. However, this has not been fully determined, and it still remains unclear whether nutrition can truly cause ADHD.

1.2.4   Smoking and Alcohol Use During
Pregnancy

Some cases of ADHD are related to the situation a kid is born into. For example, many think that drinking and smoking during pregnancy may influence a child's conduct.

There is some evidence that shows that children who are exposed to alcohol and drugs while in the womb have higher chances of developing ADHD.

1.2.5   What Doesn't Cause ADHD

There are so many myths about the cause of ADHD, and to date, when you ask professionals about the actual cause of the disorder, you'll get different answers. However, most of these answers lack any form of scientific backing even after numerous research work has been done to prove these claimed causes.

For example, many people believe that playing video games, watching TV, consuming excess sugar, poor parenting, and poverty can cause ADHD. It is important to note that these factors do not cause ADHD. They can only worsen the condition significantly.

The causes and risk factors of ADHD are still being studied, and the aim is to find a better way to reduce and manage the likelihood of a person having ADHD. The main causes and potential risk factors of ADHD include genetics, brain injury, premature delivery, alcohol use during pregnancy, low birth weight, and other environmental factors. These remain the main factors that influence ADHD development, and they all have research evidence to support the claims.

Therefore, whenever you sit and think of possible things that can cause ADHD, avoid thinking it's because of watching too much TV, eating too much sugar, social factors, parenting, or environmental factors like family chaos or poverty. These factors do not cause ADHD<, but they can make the symptoms worse.

1.2.6   Review of Possible Risk Factors of ADHD

As highlighted earlier, there's no definite cause or triggering factor of ADHD in children. The condition is as a result of so many factors, all of which contribute differently to further increase the risk of the condition:

1. **Altered function or anatomy of the brain:** Brain scans of areas on the brain that relates to attention spans and other similar activities are different among children with ADHD. Attention deficit hyperactivity disorder (ADHD) has been shown to affect people's frontal lobe levels instead of those who do not have the condition. Researchers believe that the frontal lobe is associated with decision-making and other brain processesNeurotransmitters like noradrenaline and dopamine in the brain act as chemical messengers.

2. **Being Male:** Boys and men are at greater risk of developing ADHD than women and girls. This is mainly because of hormonal or genetic factors. However, the inattentive type of ADHD is often missed out, implying that a sizeable number of girls who have ADHD may be unaccounted for

3. **Genetics:** Studies have revealed that ADHD can be inherited, and there are genes associated to cause ADHD.
4. **Traumatic Brain Injury:** Different brain injuries have been linked to ADHD. However, there are only a few children who have suffered brain injury compared to the increasing number of patients with ADHD.
5. **Food Intolerance:** Some foods may increase the risk of ADHD, and examples of these foods include nuts, wheat, and milk.
6. **Other Risk Factors:** Premature birth, exposure to television, sugar, and additives are all linked with ADHD because they can increase the risk of the disorder.

1.3   Signs and Symptoms of ADHD

One of the common things with neurodevelopmental diseases is that they exhibit signs and symptoms that can be exhibited in everybody. This is a major reason why when these signs and symptoms are exhibited by kids, parents tend to believe that they are just being stubborn and pay less attention to it.

The first thing that comes to mind whenever people think of ADHD is a child that's not easy to control. A kid that disrupts everyone and is always hyperactive. However, the condition is more complex than it may seem. Some kids with ADHD exhibit only the hyperactivity symptoms, while others remain very quiet. Some also require so much effort for them to be able to stay focused on a task or any activity.

These signs and symptoms of ADHD will depend on the dominant characteristics that are present in a child. In general, children with ADHD may show one of the following:
- Hyperactive, impulsive, and inattentive which is the most common form of ADHD.
- Inattentive, but not impulsive or hyperactive
- Impulsive and Hyperactive, but unable to pay attention

Very little attention is given to children with inattentive symptoms, and this is because they are usually calm and not disruptive. However, inattention also has its consequences, which include underperforming in school, inability to follow teachers or parent's directions, and clashing with other kids in school.

1.3.1　　Identifying ADHD at Different Ages

It is totally expected for young children to be hyperactive and easily distractible. However, the main things that stand out are the impulsive behaviors that they show. For example, blurting out insults or dangerous climbing are behaviors that stand out in kids with ADHD. In most cases, when a child is up to five years, they learn how to sit quietly, pay attention, and follow instructions. Therefore, when these kids reach school age, it becomes a lot easier to identify those with ADHD because they stand out in the three behaviors: hyperactivity, impulsivity, and inattentiveness.

1.3.1.1　Inattentiveness in ADHD

It is important to note that the main issue is not that children do not know how to pay attention. No, that's not the case. You'll often notice that they do not have issues with doing things that they enjoy or are interested in. Focusing on such tasks is as easy as anything for these kids. However, with boring or repetitive tasks, these kids find it extremely difficult to stay focused, and they tune out.

These kids do not know how to stay on other tasks, and you'll often see them bouncing from one task to another, yet they never complete any task because they are unable to stay focused. Also, these kids are not always able to organize their time or even their schoolwork. Concentration is an issue. The fascinating thing is that such kids are usually calm and quiet, and you'd think nothing is wrong with them.

1.3.1.1.1　Symptoms of Inattention in Children

Children with inattentiveness usually exhibit one of the following:

1. Do not listen when spoken to

2. Frequently misplace or lose toys, books, homework, or other items.
3. Find it hard to stay focused because they are easily distracted and get bored with tasks.
4. Do not always complete tasks.
5. Difficulty following instructions or remembering things.
6. Makes careless mistakes, and do not pay attention to details

1.3.1.2 Hyperactivity in ADHD

Hyperactivity remains the most obvious sign of ADHD, and it is usually shown in most children with the disorder. Some kids will remain quiet and still, but kids with ADHD are always on the move. You'll see them trying to do so many things at once, and they are usually quick to move from one activity to the other. It is also difficult to get these kids to remain in one position. They will either shake their legs, tap their feet, or drum with their fingers.

1.3.1.2.1 Symptoms of Hyperactivity in Children

Children with hyperactivity usually exhibit one of the following:
1. Have a quick temper
2. Always talking
3. Constantly moving, climbing, or running
4. Unable to play quietly, relax or sit still
5. Constantly fidgets.

1.3.1.3 Impulsivity in ADHD

Impulsivity can cause children to have issues with self-control. Sometimes, a kid may thin they are lesser than their friends and colleagues, and you'll see them invading people's space, interrupting conversations, and asking questions that are not relevant. Such kids usually ask overly personal questions. Asking these kids to exercise patience or wait a little longer is almost always impossible because they'll never follow it.

Another way you can easily identify children that show impulsivity symptoms is with their mood. They are usually moody and emotionally overreact to things. You might want to think that these kids are needy, weird, or disrespectful, but that's never the case.

1.3.1.3.1 Symptoms of Impulsivity in Children

Children with impulsivity usually exhibit the following:
1. Unable to keep emotion in check. Usually have emotional outbursts and tantrums
2. Often interrupt others and say things at the wrong time
3. Act irrationally and without thinking
4. Prefer guessing instead of devoting time to solve problems. They blurt out answers even when they are not called to answer a question.
5. Intrude conversations.

1.3.2 Symptoms at Different Ages

You can know all the symptoms of ADHD and how they are presented and still not be able to identify these symptoms in kids of different ages. This is because everyone can act in a way that's a lot similar to how an ADHD patient would act. However, adults and kids with ADHD usually struggle with these behaviors more than other people.

In general, adults and kids with ADHD are impulsive, have trouble managing emotions and focusing, start tasks but never finish them, or have difficulty remembering things. In addition to all of these, some people are hyperactive.

ADHD signs play out differently in different ages, and you'll find out these from the list below:

1.3.2.1 Symptoms of ADHD in Preschool-grade 2 Kids
- Fidgeting, getting up, talking unnecessary, even during quiet activities
- Unable to follow directions
- Difficulty remembering things, even what the teacher just taught. Sometimes it can be as hard as remember that $2 + 2 = 4$
- Unable to do things slowly
- Get angry or upset easily, even over minor things
- Taking things without permission

1.3.2.2 Symptoms of ADHD in Grades 3-7 Kids
- Unable to follow directions, especially if they are more than one steps
- Doing or saying things irrationally
- Rushing through homework and making careless mistakes
- Take longer time to finish assignments, even the simplest of them
- Clowning around and trying to get the attention of everyone in the class
- Always restless during school assemblies or field trips, especially if they are not really interesting

1.3.2.3 Symptoms of ADHD in Teens and Adults
- Unable to make friends easily
- Difficulty keeping track of deadlines, and unable to write down assignments
- Do not think about the consequences of their actions
- Show no interests in tasks that they feel are rather boring
- Spacing out when reading or during other similar activities
- Usually need to read information more than once or may ask people to repeat what they've said regularly

All the symptoms of ADHD usually are usually associated with emotional and academic difficulty, as well as social functioning. There are different criteria that must be met before a diagnosis can be established. ADHD may be associated with significant behavioral problems, neurological conditions, and other learning or developmental disabilities.

1.3.3   What Makes ADHD Symptoms Worse?

Depending on age, children exhibit different behaviors, and this is because the rate of development of the brain is not the same for everyone. For some people, cognitive function may be poor, while for others, it is way better. For example, a 7 year old child might have the abilities of a 10 years old child, even though another 10 year old child lacks such abilities. Therefore, you should note that the problem may not be that the ADHD is only getting worse, but it could be that the abilities of your child are not developing synchronized with their age.

Even though ADHD may not be getting worse, the tasks the kid is expected to perform tends to be more complicated for their age and surrounding circumstances like increased academic demands, and as such, certain problematic behaviors only become more problematic.For example, a child getting lower grade because they didn't submit their assignment on time.

Other complications include:

- **Performing tasks and challenges without enough support:** One common thing with school settings is that there's always a new and sometimes complex challenge for students. As children advance through school, their academic assignments become more complex, and they'd have to start studying more chapters, and writing more reports. The complexity in math, spelling, reading, and even when interacting with other students can become a problem for kids, especially if the child is unable to meet these demands. For a child with ADHD, the struggle will be more, especially if the child gets no collateral support from teachers and parents.

- **Kids often get punished for actions beyond their control:** The actions of children with ADHD are often misunderstood by teachers and parents, and they are usually criticized and, in some cases, punished by their teachers and parents. These kids may even be looked down on because of their consistent inability to complete tasks or at least remember their schoolwork. Some children with ADHD may not know how to play with their friends.

- **Problems with thinking, behaviors, and emotions:** People with ADHD often face other psychiatric disorders like anxiety and depression. Children are about 65% more likely to have other comorbid disorders with ADHD.

- **Stress:** There are several things that could stress a person with ADHD. This includes domestic violence, medical illnesses, or even the loss of a family member or friend. All these can increase the level of stress in the life of a person living with ADHD.

1.4   Types of ADHD

The Diagnostic and Statistical Manual of Mental Disorders (DSM-5) is used worldwide by psychologists to determine, diagnose, and treat individuals with ADHD. The DSM-IV (1994) and the DSM-IV TR (2000) said that individuals with ADHD were characterized by their inability to regulate their hyperactivity, inattention, and impulsivity compared to their peers of the same age and sex.

Children with ADHD usually have difficulty with staying attentive, especially to dull, repetitive, and boring activities, but tend to be active, fidgety, and restless when performing other activities.

Impulsivity is observed whenever these kids are made to focus on objectives, especially those involving more immediate gratification and rewards. A person must exhibit at least six hyperactivity-impulsivity symptoms and six inattention symptoms to be diagnosed with ADHD. Although six or more signs are needed to diagnose, these symptoms may come from either the hyperactivity-impulsivity or inattention domains. Therefore, individuals with this kind of ADHD are seen as having a mixed type of ADHD.

Therefore, when an individual meets the criteria for inattention alone, the individual is said to be Predominantly inattentive, and the same applies to individuals who meet the hyperactivity-impulsivity alone, in which they are said to be predominantly hyperactivity-impulsivity.

Barkley, in the Third Edition of his Attention-Deficit/Hyperactivity Disorder, highlights that the predominantly hyperactive-impulsive type ADHD that is evidenced in most kids may be conceptualized better as an early manifestation of a central deficit in inhibition of certain behaviors. This implies that a vast majority of kids who are viewed as hyperactive may actually be inattentive also.

The tricky thing about ADHD, especially the combined type, is that as a child grows, the symptoms of hyperactivity usually decline, but then a new issue becomes noticeable, and that's inattention. These kids are no longer hyperactive as they grow, but completing tasks becomes a lot harder. Most experts are of the opinion that the predominantly inattentive type of ADHD is completely different from the combined type. That is because of the presenting features of patients with either of the two types of ADHD.

It is not always easy to tell whether a child has ADHD or not. In most cases, kids with ADHD are often mistaken because they mimic the normal challenges that come with childhood, and this includes learning to pay attention and periods of hyperactivity. However, a child with ADHD will exhibit more severe and persistent display of a typical kid behavior, and this is as a result of the neurological differences in the brain.

One thing you should note is that your child is not ignoring you or misbehaving on purpose. It may be because the child has ADHD and doesn't know how to take turns, follow directions, sit still, or maintain focus. All this can also be attributed to the neurological deficits of the brain, which is part of what causes ADHD.

Most parents do not usually know if their child has ADHD or not, and this is because they do not fully know the types of ADHD, let alone the symptoms of each type. From all that's mentioned from the beginning of this chapter to this very point, and from a medical and general point of view, there are three types of ADHD. These types include the following:

1.4.1 Inattentive Type ADHD

While ADHD represents attention-deficit/hyperactivity disorder, there are some children that only battle with attention deficit rather than the full disorder. This type of ADHD is referred to as the inattentive presentation.

Children with this kind of ADHD are often scattered, and it is challenging for them to finish assignments, do well in school, or handle their household duties. In addition to all the other challenges these youngsters face, staying focused is also a difficult job. A kid must show at least six of the following symptoms to be diagnosed with the inattentive form of ADHD:

1. Frequently forget daily activities, especially chores
2. Does not care about details and frequently makes errors without concern.
3. Easily distracted by their thoughts or things in the environment

4. Unable to pay attention to tasks, even for playtime activities
5. Loses things frequently, like toys, books, eyeglasses, and school assignments
6. Doesn't listen when you speak to them. You'll notice that their mind is always on something else
7. Dislikes tasks and often avoid tasks, especially those that require mental effort like reading or homework
8. Unable to stay organized
9. Difficulty following instructions, and never completes schoolwork or chores.

Knowing these inattentive behaviors is important, but what's more important is known where they cross the line from the typical behavior of a child to that of a child with ADHD. Here's the best guideline:

When the inattentive behavior starts to interfere with social or family life, or when the behavior adversely affects performance in school. You'll need to get your child screened for ADHD if you notice this.

1.4.2   Hyperactivity and Impulsivity Type ADHD

Your child may be great when it comes to paying attention but having serious issues when it comes to impulsivity and hyperactivity. On the other hand, a kid that exhibits hyperactivity doesn't always have ADHD. He/She must demonstrate six signs of inattention for every diagnosis of ADHD. These symptoms include the following:

1. Always interrupt or jump abruptly into games, even when not invited.

2. Unable to sit still, tapping hands or feet regularly, and often squirming
3. Not patient, and unable to wait to take their turn
4. Often leave seat, even when they are supposed to stay put
5. Talks excessively
6. Climb or run inappropriately
7. Always on the go
8. Difficulty playing quietly
9. Blurt out answers even before a question or sentence is complete

The hyperactivity-impulsivity type and inattentive type ADHD have so many symptoms in common with each other. ADHD also occurs with other common developmental disabilities like autism.

1.4.3   Combined Type ADHD

The third type of ADHD that's also diagnosed in children is the combined type. Children with this type of ADHD exhibit features of both the hyperactivity-impulsivity and the inattentive types of ADHD. When both types are present, the combined type of ADHD is diagnosed in these kids.

The National Institutes of Health identifies this type of ADHD as the most common type of ADHD in kids, with hyperactivity being a predominant feature among preschool-age children. However, this doesn't mean everyone has ADHD. It is totally normal for the attention to wander, but the frequency of this is what makes the difference. The thoughts of people with ADHD wanders too frequently, in addition to other severe symptoms that can negatively impact day to day life.

1.5 A breakdown of ADHD behavior compared to normal behavior

ADHD represents Attention Deficit Hyperactivity Disorder. It's a neurodevelopmental dysfunction that affects people, primarily children's behavior. However, it could be persistent to adulthood. It is usually characterized by inattentiveness, hyperactivity, and impulsiveness. The goal of this chapter is to explore how this characterized behavior compares to normal behavior. For context, it's best to define what a 'normal behavior' is. Normal or normality is a relative term as it is influenced by culture, place, time, and even personal experiences such as expression of emotions resulting from loss of loved one could make one behavior seemingly abnormal. Abnormal or pathological behavior is defined as one that violates social norms, is maladaptive, is uncommon given the surrounding culture and environment, and causes the individual a lot of pain in their everyday life according to the DSM-5. The flipped side of this definition gives us a clue to what is normal. Furthermore, a breakdown of ADHD behavior and how it compares to normal behavior would be best explained under the following subheadings, namely;

1.5.1   Inattention

Inattention is the inability to concentrate or attend to a particular task meticulously. For instance, Roy is a five-year-old boy based in Illinois, Chicago, U.S. Roy is currently in kindergarten at a school 1km away from where he lives. It was in the middle of the fall class when a project that every member of the class would execute was announced. His teacher, Mrs. Ella, had specific instructions on how this project should be done. Roy seems not to be getting it even after being told the specifics repeatedly. He would rather do the opposite. Aside from this, Mrs. Ella has observed Roy's inability to keep to instruction; at first peep, it all seems to be too much energy which Mrs. Ella admired. However, when it became persistent and recurrent, Mrs. Ella became even more worried. Again, it was a struggle for Roy to organize his toys into his toy pack; he frequently had more than one missing set in his toy pack. Roy liked to try a lot of activities but never reached the climax of any of the activities. He seems quite distracted and uninterested in activities that his mate was delighted in.

Could this be a disorder or just mere apathy, Mrs. Ella often pondered to herself. Roy needed help. It was hard for Mrs. Ella to distinguish between normal child behavior and abnormal child behavior. It suddenly appeared to be pathologic to her when she took her observations to Roy's parents, and Roy's parents had the same things to say of Roy. The psychiatrist report proved the patient fear- ADHD. Moreover, the question remains. How does this behavior compare to normal behavior? How would a normal Child behave? Should there be an underlying discord such as anger, stress, and family issues, etc.? A normal Child with the underlying issues mentioned above is not expected to behave absurdly for a period longer than six months. However, in ADHD, this behavior would persist until adulthood if preventive measures are not employed. A normal Child within Roy's age is often eager to learn, try new things till it's finished. At the same time, an ADHD patient has difficulties staying and seeing through a project because they are constantly bombarded with thoughts instantaneously such as what do I eat this evening, what color of clothes should I wear. According to James

Another adult-like scenario of an ADHD patient is Mr. Walter, a sales executive at a multinational company in California, U. S. On a bright and eventful afternoon after a few meetings in the conference Hall of the company. Mr. Walter, walking down a stair at work, sights Mr. Jesse, a human resource manager at the same company, waves his hand in an attempt to greet and compliment Mr. Jesse. Mr. Jesse, who seems to be busy, lifted his face off the piece of paper in his hand, responded to Mr. Walter rather more swiftly, and continued with his work. This is a normal event that could occur in a busy and tense workplace. A normal person would interpret the signal from Mr. Walter as a show of busyness and carry on with his normal work. However, an ADHD patient like Mr. Walter gets back to his office, over-analyzing what has happened, wondering persistently if he has offended Mr. Jesse or any of his colleagues before the occurrence of this event. He thinks deeply about whether his look or smell prompted that response. This excessive concern about Mr. Jesse's response delays the project he was supposed to handle and affected the outcome of the overall sales. Again, Mr. Walter is unable to sleep because series of events that relate and are unrelated to the event that happened previously keeps his eyes open and restless. People without ADHD feel this way at the time; nonetheless, the difference is that a normal person may interpret this experience simply and move on to carry out his duty, but the reverse is the case for an ADHD patient. A lack of willpower does not cause ADHD. It is caused by the fact that the brain is wired incorrect.

Another instance of inattention in ADHD can be seen in Miss Jane, a twenty-three-year-old graduate student at an ivy league University. She sits in her class of 15 Students paying attention to her professor with skin like the color of chocolate. She listens to the lecture as everyone else, suddenly, she starts to think of work, family, supper, and what the boyfriend said two night ago when they met at the University's courtyard. She looks to throw the window and sees a young boy picking some bar of chocolate that fell off his hand, and now she is wondering what kind of care parent the boy has that left him to wander alone. Suddenly, the lecture hall manager walks into the Hall with a more temporary marker for the lecturer. She almost immediately starts analyzing the choice of colors the hall manager brought and wondering if it was right or not. Her attention comes back to what the lecturer is saying then again wanders away from time to time.

Similarly, Miss Jane manages to study for her midterms; she was very prepared and ready to take her test. Before the test, her flatmate Miss Evelyn quizzed her, and she seems to remember everything she has read; however, on reaching the exam Hall, she cannot remember a single bit of what she has studied and learned. She missed the quiz and failed the course.

These and more are some of the things people with ADHD deal with. They tend to lack the ability to focus on a particular course as well as remember things when they are most needed. Moreover, a person without ADHD can get him or herself to focus regardless of how boring or interesting the course is, moreover, for an ADHD patient. If it's not interesting to him, he can not focus on that.

Download the Audio Book Version of This Book for FREE

If you love listening to audio books on-the-go, I have great news for you. You can download the audio book version of this book for **FREE** just by signing up for a **FREE** 30-day Audible trial! See below for more details!

As an audible customer, you will receive the below benefits with your 30-day free trial:

- FREE audible book copy of this book
- After the trial, you will get 1 credit each month to use on any audiobook
- Your credits automatically roll over to the next month if you don't use them
- Choose from Audible's 200,000 + titles
- Listen anywhere with the Audible app across multiple devices
- Make easy, no-hassle exchanges of any audiobook you don't love
- Keep your audiobooks forever, even if you cancel your membership

Click the links below to get started!

For Audible US
https://www.audible.com/pd/B09NNS88XD/?source_code=AUDFPWS0223189MWT-BK-ACX0-290151&ref=acx_bty_BK_ACX0_290151_rh_us

For Audible UK
https://www.audible.co.uk/pd/B09NNR39Z9/?source_code=AUKFrDlWS02231890H6-BK-ACX0-290151&ref=acx_bty_BK_ACX0_290151_rh_uk

For Audible FR:
https://www.audible.fr/pd/B09NNSXS58/?source_code=FRAORWS022318903B-BK-ACX0-290151&ref=acx_bty_BK_ACX0_290151_rh_fr

For Audible DE
https://www.audible.de/pd/B09NNSSQ1T/?source_code=EKAORWS0223189009-BK-ACX0-290151&ref=acx_bty_BK_ACX0_290151_rh_de

1.5.2 Hyperactivity and impulsiveness

Hyperactivity is a state of being restless and always abnormally active. It's a state of being beyond control. This is a characteristic of ADHD, and it's seen in Mr. Richard, a sports analyst. Mr. Richard made a reservation in a restaurant, where he was looking forward to having an amazing time with Miss. Zita is a newly employed accountant in his office. Mr. Richard arrives first and takes others on behalf of Miss Zita. Just as the waitress delivered the order, Miss Zita worked in looking all glamorous. Shortly, they started eating and talking Intermittently. Mr. Richard happened to hear an obnoxious sound while Miss Zita chewed some of the nuts on the table. Mr. Richard became infuriated and irritated and clinched his hand. In an attempt to hit Miss Zita, he immediately remembered he didn't want to go to jail. He didn't carry out his thoughts. In normal people, these obnoxious sounds may just have been unnoticeable. Mr. Richard almost acted out of impulse for something unnecessary. Thanks to his fear of jail.

Again, ADHD patients tend to worry more about things going on around them. For instance, Mr. Richard, while returning home from an unexpectedly distasteful dinner, is on a three Lane express road. He is in a Toyota Camry car in the middle lane, and he has a fuel tanker on his left delivery to a gas station, and on his right, he has a truck full of wood. All these vehicles were moving at almost the same mile per hour. Then suddenly, the anxiety of Mr. Richard spikes. He is worried that something may just happen, how the two vehicles may just crush his car, leaving him to bleed to death before the emergency response team arrives. Suddenly he is sweating profusely and almost mistakenly hit the truck on the right. It's normal for a person to have such a level of anxiety. However, when this level of worry is persistent, it becomes pathologic.

ADHD can be likened to Depression; everyone feels down at some point in their life; therefore, the difference between a clinically depressed person and a technically depressed person is that in the clinical stage, the depressive symptoms become recurrent and affect the person's daily activities or routine adversely.

ADHD is often not noticeable in childhood because there may be a parent that helps them organize things or teachers that help them out with organization and time management. However, when these people move to college, where they have everything from classes, extracurricular activities, and social activities to plan for themselves, they become confused, therefore, may begin to exhibit the signs of ADHD. Mr. Robins, a freshman student at a state University in the United States of America. Has recently been diagnosed with ADHD. Before this diagnosis, he was known to always interrupt the class. He would bring up a sports report in a class currently talking about anaerobes in the Microbiology class. This was surprising to everyone in the class, and some students reacted irritated and disdainfully. Again, he would constantly fidget as though he has a cube of ice under his clothes.

Nonetheless, he was good at the University's volleyball and found it hard to focus in class. He was always distracted and yell when he felt saturated with ideas. He also had no friends because no one could put up with his inconsistent behavior. It was also reported that Mr. Robins would never wait for his turn at the dining hall; this almost leads to a fight on campus. Thanks to the security man on duty that day, he intervened intelligibly. This helped curbed the conflict that would have resulted from Mr. Robin's lack of patients. Of course, a normal person might behave in a way that might be compared to Mr. Robin's own, especially in stress and pressure. However, a normal person won't do it consistently and wouldn't like to put himself in danger of school penalties. His diagnosis of ADHD made a difference in the way people reacted to him. They saw him as a sick person who needed help. Hence, they become even more supportive. His school health insurance provided all the psychotherapy and drugs he needed to support him.

In conclusion, ADHD is not a male disease, though males are most diagnosed, and it affects all ages that could persist from childhood to adulthood. The symptoms of ADHD are often very similar to Normal behavior. However, the difference is in the frequency of manifestation of this symptom. For instance, abnormal reactions resulting from stress and emotional states may be termed normal behavior, but if these behaviors are persistent and recurrent, impairing the patient's activities, it could be classified as a pathologic behavior. This disorder is mostly inherited.

1.6 ADHD Diagnosis and Differential Diagnosis

ADHD is a neurodevelopmental dysfunction that affects both males and females, although males are most diagnosed. This dysfunction affects behavior adversely and makes it uneasy for people with ADHD to socialize with their peers as their behavior is interpreted as weird. It affects people of all ages ranging from children to adults. However, there is no single test for diagnosing ADHD, unlike conventional diseases like malaria that you would have to do microscopy to identify the parasite and its absence or presence defines the diagnosis. For ADHD, imaging of the brain, X-ray has proved ineffective, even though it gives insight to the Attention Deficit Hyperactivity Disorder patient's brain wiring. They are drugs that improve ADHD symptoms in individuals. However, these drugs are just like someone who has an impaired leg may be due to accidents and uses a walking aid. If you take the walking aide away, his immobility continues, but he normally locomotes the walking aide. Treatment with methylphenidate, including Ritalin, Methylin, and Concerta, is an excellent example of this kind of medication (Focalin). Additionally, someone who has lost a loved one or is in crisis can display the same symptoms as someone who has Attention Deficit Hyperactivity Disorder. Therefore, special care should be taken to identify and differentiate normal reactions to stressful events from Attention Deficit Hyperactivity Disorder symptoms.

To diagnose ADHD, a person must notify the individual's behavior and compare it to that of a typical person of their age.ADHD is found in people of all ages, basically, childhood and adulthood. Therefore, the diagnosis for ADHD has been classified into two, namely;

1.6.1 Diagnosis of ADHD

Following the guidelines of the CDC (Centre for Disease Control and Prevention), children from two years old have been diagnosed with Attention Deficit Hyperactivity Disorder. Diagnosis of this neurodevelopmental dysfunction in children falls heavily on the patient, the parent, the teacher if the patient is in school, and also a social worker carries out the evaluation with expertise in ADHD (Attention Deficit Hyperactivity Disorder). The parent's answers to the evaluator (social worker) as regards any history of ADHD in the family also produce information on their child's behavior at home and the community.

Early infancy, developmental milestones, allergies, hunger, sleep habits, height, weight, and hospitalization are factors for which the parent should take responsibility. Again, reports must be gathered from the child's teacher if he or she is in school. The role of the teacher here is to make a report on the child's performance in terms of grades, extracurricular and how well the child socializes with others. The essence of this report from parents and teachers is to develop a plan that helps the child cope with ADHD, if any. For a child to be diagnosed with ADHD, he or she must meet specific criteria stipulated by DSM- 5. These criteria are divided into two based on the two types of ADHD: inattentiveness and hyperactivity and impulsivity. He or she must meet six of nine criteria in one or both types of ADHD; however, for teenagers of 17 and above, at least five of the symptoms are required.

1.6.2 The symptoms of each list are;

1. **Inattentiveness**: For inattention, the kid must have at least six symptoms of nine persistently for six months and above, and this symptom must have been proven to have affected the child adversely. According to the DSM-5, people with Inattentive form of ADHD will suffer from the following symptoms:

a) Makes thoughtless errors in schooling, at employment, or at other activities by failing to pay careful attention to details.

b) Frequently struggles to maintain concentration on work or recreational activities (tends to become distracted when in class, in discussions, or while reading).

c) When talked to directly, he often does not seem to listen (While there is no apparent source of distraction, the mind appears elsewhere).

d) Frequently ignores directions and fails to complete homework, housework, or job responsibilities (gets things done, yet easily becomes distracted and gets side-tracked).

e) Has a hard time coordinating chores and activities (is troubled with sequential tasks; fails to keep items and resources organised; messy, disorganised routine).

f) Rather than bear the mental strain, he prefers to skip the job entirely (preparing reports, filling out forms, and reading long papers are examples of schooling or homework for older teens and adults).

g) The individual often loses items that are essential for activities or duties (keys, identity card, documents, school supplies, mobile phone, books and eyeglasses).

h) has a hard time focusing on one task when faced with several distractions (may involve irrelevant ideas for older teens and adults).

i) It often makes mistakes in everyday tasks (chores, doing errands, answering phone calls, paying bills, and maintaining appointments for older adolescents and adults).

2. **Hyperactivity and Impulsivity**: To be diagnosed with this type of ADHD, six or more symptoms must be persistent and Known to severe daily or routine living. The DSM-5 criteria for a mental disorder, for example, include:

- He/She will fidget often, tapping his hands, tapping his feet, or fidgeting in his seat.

- In circumstances when being seated is required, he often departs his seat. (workplace, classroom, dinner).

- Frequently goes about or climbs in places where it is not acceptable (these behaviors are limited in adolescents and adults).

- She/He cannot or cannot remain uncomfortable for a long time, such at restaurants or meeting for example.

- The person speaks a much.

- The response is often blurred before an inquiry is finished (Completes the phrases of others; cannot wait for a conversation turn).

- Often it's hard to wait for its turn.

It's also important for the follow-up to be conducted should the child meet the criteria. The social worker may provide an option for you to explore medication or therapy. Coexisting symptoms like anger, depression, and anxiety should be evaluated as well.

1.6.3   Differential diagnosis of ADHD (Attention Deficit Hyperactivity Disorder.

Many underlying dysfunctions exhibits Attention Deficit Hyperactivity Disorder symptoms, which poses a challenge to truly diagnosing ADHD. Examples of such neurologic dysfunction are dyslexia, anxiety disorder, sleep disturbance (apnea), oppositional defiant disorder, substance abuse. When this dysfunction are been ruled out, it makes it easier to diagnosis ADHD.

Attention Deficit Hyperactivity Disorder is often accompanied by other underlying dysfunctions, making accurate diagnosis difficult. For example, oppositional defiant disorder, substance abuse, anxiety disorder and learning problems are all forms of brain dysfunction (dyslexia). To help with the diagnosis of ADHD, we can rule out this problem.

Anxiety disorder

Anxiety is a physiological coping mechanism that the brain undergoes during stress. However, anxiety disorder is a mental illness associated with constant fear. Anxiety can make one perform poorly in school, relationships, and in Socializing with others. Anxiety can make someone inattentive and even hyperactive, which are classic symptoms of ADHD. Therefore, it's critical to rule out anxiety disorders from ADHD. Panic disorder is a type of anxiety disorder that can cause the patient to behave in a certain way that supports forgetfulness, fidgeting, and inability to join in tasks and activities requiring executive function.

Sleep disturbance

Sleep is an essential activity need to keep the tissues, organs, and other body structures running. Sleep plays a bunch of roles in cognition, memory, toxic removal, emotional regulations, to mention but a few. Sleep disturbance can lead to hypoxia during the night, which culminates in unrefreshed feelings and affects concentration. Research shows that people who experience sleep disturbance are likely to be inattentive and make silly mistakes because the prefrontal cortex that is useful in executive function, has been deprived of rest. Therefore, these parameters should be ruled out in the diagnosis of ADHD.

Substances abuse

Excessive consumption of alcohol, cannabis, and other illicit substances affects cognition adversely since they will not attend to their environment. And so they begin to manifest symptoms similar to ADHD. This should be ruled out in diagnosis too.

What's the Oppositional Defiant Disorder (ODD)?

This is a disorder in which someone displays obstinate defiance, spite, discourtesy, and contempt for legitimate authority. Every human being has had an emotional outburst, whether it was intentional or not. However, if this behavior is persistent and disrupting the other surrounding users of the community's tranquility, it could be suggestive of ODD.

Let's talk about the Conduct disorder

This is a behavioral defect characterized by a disregard for people and violence, and no manners. This kind of character is evident in children and adolescents. An ADHD patient with hyperactivity and impulsiveness may possess this kind of defect since they don't think through before they respond to stimuli. Children with this defect are often hostile to other kids in school and social gatherings.

Learning Difficulty

It's very easy to confuse someone who cannot read and write for ADHD because the individual cannot concentrate, leading to this. There are three types of learning difficulties, namely;

- Dyslexia (difficulty with reading)

- Dysgraphia (difficulty with write)

- Dyscalculia (difficulty with math)

People with learning difficulties are not dumb. However, their brains are wired to make them see things differently from popular view, which is what makes the difference.

In summary, Parents, teachers, and social workers who are experts in ADHD must identify the problem a kid faces and use methods to help relieve the pain. As a matter of fact, there is no specific direct assessment for ADHD, the best approach is to interview using the Diagnostic and Statistical Manual of Mental Disorders,(DSM- 5th edition) criteria. Again, certain forms of behavioural dysfunction, such as depression, anxiety, sleep disturbances, drug addiction, and ODD/CD co-occur or co-exist with ADHD. The parameters must be carefully distinguished from ADHD. An adult from seventeen years old and above should meet at least five of ten symptoms in one or both of the criteria. Also, children and adolescents should meet six of the nine criteria in one or both criteria to be diagnosed with ADHD.

1.7 Comorbidities

People with ADHD have co-existing illnesses, whether known or concealed. Depression, anxiety, or another learning impairment are the most common reasons for the disease. In order to enhance the quality of life for your kid, many secondary disorders will require specific therapy.

How then do you identify these conditions and differentiate the symptoms? Could it be ADHD or just another related condition with a similar symptom? For an individual with only ADHD, the treatment will be a life-changer, and in most cases, a stimulant or a nonstimulant may be used in addition to other behavioral therapy, exercise, and dietary changes. A combination of these can help to significantly improve the symptoms of hyperactivity, impulsivity, and distractibility.

Even though these treatment options are effective, it is often observed that some people still experience other significant symptoms like defiance, learning problems, organization problems, and deep sadness, even after the ADHD symptoms are completely under control. For example, Mark, a seven year old child, is diagnosed with ADHD. The doctor then placed him on an effective stimulant, and within a very short time, the parent noticed a significant improvement in the ADHD symptoms he normally exhibits. However, there was still an issue of concern. Mark was still struggling with his classwork, and his parents weren't happy with that. It became as if only the hyperactivity decreased and every other thing reduced.

Whenever a challenge is noticed after ADHD is treated, it serves as a clue to an undiagnosed condition that was existing alongside ADHD.

Several years ago, doctors only considered ADHD as a standalone condition, but they were wrong to think this way because more than 50% of people with ADHD tend to have one or more underlying conditions. This is also referred to as comorbidities, and ADHD comorbidities include the following:

- Tic disorders
- Depression
- Executive function difficulties
- Learning disabilities
- Find and gross motor difficulties
- Language disabilities
- Anxiety
- Oppositional defiant disorder
- Obsessive-compulsive disorder
- Other neurological or psychological problems

A Comorbid Condition is Usually Due to ADHD, In Which Case It Could Be Triggered by the Stress of Managing ADHD Symptoms.

Chronic unfocusedness, like in the case of a girl, will make her feel more worried at school. It is well known that if a woman with undiagnosed ADHD has been dealing with years of negative feedback or even rejection, she may develop depression. In some cases, the secondary problem will fade once the symptoms of ADHD are brought under control, but that's not always the case, and whenever this problem is not resolved, it's an indication of a comorbid condition.

I've mentioned comorbid conditions a couple of times already. Here's what it actually means.

1.7.1   What is a Comorbid Condition?

A comorbid condition is a distinct condition that exists concurrently with another disorder, like ADHD. These conditions don't resolve as soon as the primary condition does, and the case is similar with ADHD. ADHD exists with other comorbid conditions, and they often require specific treatment plans.

A child diagnosed with a comorbid condition may require psychotherapy, school accommodations, or other medications in addition to the treatment already received for ADHD.

1.7.2   Common ADHD Comorbidity Categories

A peculiar thing about ADHD comorbidity is that the conditions are usually diagnosed in a similar fashion, and they exist along a similar spectrum of severity, which is from mild to severe. The symptoms vary with their causes, and it often includes environmental toxins, prenatal trauma, genes, and more.

1. Cortical Wiring Problems

Structural anomalies in the brain area and cerebral cortex lead to issues with cortical wiring. The cortical wiring problems that exist as comorbid continues are:
- Executive function difficulties
- Fine and gross motor difficulties
- Language disabilities
- Learning disabilities

These problems can be treated with lifestyle changes and academic accommodations. It is important to note that medications are not effective for treating cortical wiring problems.

2. Problems Regulating Emotions

This is also a comorbid condition that occurs simultaneously with ADHD, and people with this problem often experience the following:
- Bipolar disorder
- Obsessive-compulsive disorder
- Anger-control problems
- Anxiety disorders
- Depression

Depression is a peculiar emotional problem that can cause other symptoms beyond suicidal thoughts and sadness. Depression can also reduce a child's interest in different activities, even the most pleasurable. Other symptoms include irritability, feeling of worthlessness, slowness or agitation, loss of energy, inappropriate anger, inability to concentrate, and more.

Certain medication groups like selective serotonin reuptake inhibitors can be used in managing regulatory problems. These medications are sometimes used alongside other ADHD medications.

For bipolar disorders, there are so many possible treatments that could be used. A psychiatrist must know how to administer medications for ADHD alongside bipolar disorder.

3. Tic Disorders

This disorder is characterized by sudden twitches or muscles. Tic disorders vary in their severity, and they usually include:

- Tourette's syndrome
- Oral tics
- Motor tics

1.7.3   Differentiating Symptoms of ADHD from ADHD Comorbidity

If you notice that your child continues to struggle with their symptoms, even after they've started receiving treatment for ADHD, you might want to determine the symptoms that are secondary to ADHD or identify whether it's a comorbid disorder or not. There's currently no almighty test that can be used to determine this, and the best thing to do is to perform a differential diagnosis. To start a differential diagnosis, you'll need to carefully observe when and where each symptom arises.

1. **Secondary problems usually begin at a particular time:** In some cases, they may occur only under some circumstances. Maybe you noticed that your child started having excessive anxiety in the third grade, and she tends to be anxious when at school or even at home whenever she remembers homework. If this is the case, then it may likely be an anxiety disorder that is secondary to ADHD. This is not a comorbid condition.

2. **On the other hand, a comorbid condition can be pervasive and chronic:** They are usually obvious in childhood and may extend deep into adulthood and in every situation of life. These conditions don't occur only under certain circumstances, and they are evident in almost every other life situation. For example, a mood shift that is ADHD-related may be triggered by varying

life events. However, a mood shift that's related to bipolar disorder can only be triggered by specific life events.

1.7.4   Consult a child and adolescent psychologist or psychiatrist

Are you suspecting your child has other disorders in addition to ADHD? Then it's time to perform a critical assessment with the aim of identifying possible language, learning, executive function, learning, and organization problems. In addition to the critical assessment, a clinical evaluation by a psychiatrist will help you to identify the conditions and determine whether the child is living with anger control, tic, OCD, depression, or anxiety disorder.

1.7.5   What Are the Common Symptoms Associated with ADHD Comorbidities?

The list below contains different associated comorbid conditions to help you compare with the symptoms you've observed with your child. The need to recognize the symptoms early, as well as to ensure prompt intervention, cannot be overemphasized.

Learning Disabilities
- Difficulty with mastering a new academic reasoning or concept, or with memory
- Unable to master writing, math, or reading skills

Language Disabilities
- Unable to organize thoughts
- Difficult to find the right words when talking
- Unable to understand whatever is said

Executive Function Difficulties
- Unable to manage function and regulate emotions
- Difficulty recalling or remembering details
- Unable to plan and execute projects
- Difficulty organizing thoughts, especially when writing

Anxiety
- Stomach aches or headaches
- Excessive worry
- Panic attacks
- Generalized fears beyond the age of a child

Depression
- Inappropriate anger
- Sleep disturbances
- Unexplained irritability or agitation
- Feelings of worthlessness
- Decreased ability to concentrate
- Persistent loss of appetite, fatigue, or moodiness
- Unexplained feelings of guilt

Anger-control problems
- Irrational, especially during a meltdown
- Usually remorseful afterward
- Uncontrolled rage or anger, which may last for more than 30 minutes

Sensory Processing Disorder
- Muted sounds, touch, and sights
- Feeling overwhelmed by sensory stimuli like loud noises, tags, seams on clothing, strong odors, or bright lights.

Bipolar Disorder
- Excessive talking

- Mood swings
- Difficulty relaxing
- Mood shifts without any life connection

Tic Disorders
- Complex and simple vocal or motor tics

Obsessive-Compulsive Disorder (OCD)
- Need for extreme cleanliness or order
- Extreme anxiety or hypervigilance
- Goal-directed behavior
- Neet to hoard or collect object

1.8 Management of ADHD: Medication Options

In previous chapters, we have talked about ADHD (Attention Deficit Hyperactivity Disorder) in its entirety. We have looked at the causes of ADHD, the signs and symptoms of ADHD, the epidemiology, and the physiology of the disorder.

We would discuss the management of ADHD, as well as the therapy, various medications utilised, and their mechanisms of action and adverse effects in this chapter. The only medication therapy for ADHD is likely to help alleviate the symptoms.

Treatment aims to relieve symptoms and to improve day-to-day quality of life. Treatments include medications, behavioral therapy, counseling, and education services, or a combination of all for maximum impact.
The drugs used in the treatment include;
1. Methylphenidate
2. Lisdexamfetamine
3. Dexamfetamine
4. Atomoxetine
5. Guanfacine

Like earlier stated, these medicines can manage ADHD but cannot cure the disorder. Also, it is advised that you visit your doctor when you notice any side effects. Do not stop any of these drugs without talking to your doctor first. Normally, when starting these medications, patients with ADHD are placed on low doses before the doses are increased gradually.

It is worthy of note that the first-line treatment for ADHD, the Stimulants (Methylphenidate and Amphetamine derivatives), are used. Though there are other drugs, these are mostly drugs of choice when treating the disorder. Studies have shown that the use of stimulant medication in ADHD patients reduces the risk of substance abuse.

The stimulants used as first-line treatment include:

- Methylphenidate
- Amphetamine derivative (lisdexamfetamine and dexamphetamine).

1.8.1   Methylphenidate

It is a CNS stimulant. It is derived from the phenethylamine and piperidine classes. It comes in different formulations. It can be taken orally or topically.

Methylphenidate is a norepinephrine-dopamine reuptake inhibitor. Its mechanism of action is by increasing the action of the CNS by inhibiting the reuptake of neurotransmitters Dopamine and Serotonin.

This inhibition allows the neurotransmitters to stay long in the brain to increase activity. Methylphenidate increases concentration and keeps the brain occupied. The drug causes increased alertness, reduced fatigue, and a high attention span.

This drug has been considered relatively safe though it has a few side effects. Methylphenidate may have several side effects, including:

- loss of appetite
- trouble sleeping
- weight loss

- dizziness
- nausea
- vomiting
- nervousness
- headache

Are associated with the use of methylphenidate. Serious side effects associated with its use include:

- Signs of blood flow
- Irregular heartbeat
- Changes in mood and behavior
- Uncontrolled muscle movement
- Blurred vision

Get medical help immediately if you encounter any of the following:

- Symptoms of heart attack
- Symptoms of stroke
- Fainting
- Seizure.

1.8.1.1 Precautions

While using this medication, ensure you do the following;

- Check your blood pressure regularly, as it can elevate blood pressure.
- Do not administer to children below 6 yrs of age.
- Check if as a patient, you are hypersensitive to methylphenidate or other components of the drug.
- Do not use methylphenidate if, as a patient, you have used MAOI drugs in the past 14 days.

- If you have severe hypertension, high thyroid levels, glaucoma, severe anxiety, or tension, then you cannot use Methylphenidate.

Take methylphenidate as directed by your doctor. It may become a habit, but your doctor would know best. It's good with or without food. If you miss a dosage, take it as soon as you recall, but not with the next.

1.8.2 Lisdexamfetamine

This is an Amphetamine derivative. It is a stimulant drug also used in the treatment of ADHD. It is also used in the treatment of binge eating disorders in adults. It is usually less preferred to Methylphenidate.

It has been shown to benefit brain and nerve development. The medication has been in long-term use and has shown positive results for the primary symptoms of ADHD, which include inattention, hyperactivity, and impulsiveness. It also reduces the risk of substance abuse development. Research indicates that the medication has been utilised to enhance patients' overall well-being, from academic benefits to social gains.

It works by releasing the neurotransmitters in the brain from their storage sites. It also works by preventing or inhibiting the reuptake of these neurotransmitters in the brain.

It is interesting to note that Lisdexamfetamine is a prodrug that is converted to Dextroamphetamine and L-lysine in the body. Dextroamphetamine is the active form of the drug.

The common side effects of the drug are;
- Loss of appetite

- Insomnia
- Nausea
- Losing weight
- Anxiety
- Diarrhea
- Dry mouth
- Irritability
- Dizziness

Contact your doctor if you notice any of the following;
- Allergic reactions in the form of itching, rash, swelling.
- Mental issues in the form of suicidal options and the like.
- Blurred vision.
- Heart problems like chest pain, high blood pressure, and the likes.

1.8.2.1 Precautions
- The drug can cause strokes and heart problems.
- Do not take the drug with MAOI because it can increase the risk of hypertensive crisis.

Take the drug according to your Doctors prescription and advice. The drug can be habit-forming, so follow your Doctor's advice. You can also take the drug with or without food and mostly in the morning. If you have questions, be sure to consult your Doctor or Pharmacist. If you miss a dose, take it at the next available time. Do not take the missed dose together with the next dose. Remember, drugs can be efficacious but can also be poisons, so always do well to consult your Doctor or Pharmacists. Remember that an overdose of Lisdexamfetamine can be fatal, so do not overdose.

1.8.3   Dexamfetamine

It is also known as Dextroamphetamine. It is an Amphetamine derivative. Remember in the previous drug explanation; we said that Lisdexamfetamine is a prodrug, and it is metabolized in the body to give L-lysine and Dextroamphetamine. This Dextroamphetamine is the metabolite and the active substance of that prodrug. The thing with this drug is it has other health benefits apart from the treatment of ADHD.

The drug can also be used to improve athletic performance, cognitive function; it can be used as a euphoriant and aphrodisiac to give you that feeling of pleasure and make you last longer during sex. It is a known psychostimulant.

It works by inhibiting the transportation of the neurotransmitters in the CNS to their storage vesicle. Thereby making them last longer in the brain to improve brain function, increase alertness. The ultimate goal of the medication is to improve the patient's quality of life. I'd say that it hinders the transporter proteins, which use TAAR1 to carry monoamine neurotransmitters to their storage locations (Trace amine-associated receptor 1).

Normally, it is a prodrug that is usually prescribed, while dextroamphetamine is active after absorption of the prodrug. Generally, the drug is used to improve the ability to pay attention, improve focus, and improve behavioral patterns. Extra package enhances your listening skills and helps you organize your tasks.

Common side effects of the drug are:
- Headache
- Dry Mouth

- Unpleasant taste
- Weight loss, especially in children.
- Changes in sex drive
- Constipation.

Contact your doctor if you are experiencing any of the following:

- Excessive fatigue
- Mood changes
- Anxiety
- Aggressiveness
- Hallucinations
- Seizures
- Dizziness
- Blurred vision
- Slow speech
- Numbness
- It can also cause growth retardation in children using this drug for the treatment of ADHD.

1.8.3.1 Precautions

The drug should be used with caution in patients that are:

- Hypersensitive to any dextroamphetamine, lisdexamfetamine, or other component used essmanufacture.
- If you as a patient have a history of glaucoma, hypertension, high blood pressure, hyperthyroidism, bipolar disorder, depression, anxiety.
- If you are pregnant or breastfeeding.

- Tell your doctor the other medications you are taking as some can inhibit the action or decrease absorption of the drug.
- If you took MAOI within the past 14 days.

Remember to check your blood pressure regularly. It could be drowsy, so do not drive or operate heavy machinery after drug use.

Remember to consult your Doctor or Pharmacist when taking the drug. Take the drug according to your Doctors prescription. The medication is given 1–3 times day, with or without meals. Usually, the first dosage is in the am.

As stated earlier, the doctor usually prescribed low doses, and the dose can be increased with continuous use. In this case, you can take the drug 4- 6 hours apart.

1.8.4   Atomoxetine

It is a norepinephrine reuptake inhibitor. Should be taken by children that are at least 6 years in age. Normally taken orally. A unique advantage above other drugs used in ADHD treatment, is that it has little or no abuse potential. It is a non stimulant medication but can be used together with stimulant drugs to give a synergistic effect. On its own, the drug shows low response and treatment to ADHD, but it can inhibit the reuptake of these neurotransmitters.

It works by inhibiting the reuptake of the brain's neurotransmitters and also prevents the storage of the neurotransmitters.

Common side effects are;
- Loss of appetite

- Weight loss
- Constipation
- Nausea
- Vomiting
- Fatigue
- Insomnia
- In women, irregular menses may occur
- Decreased libido and sexual activity.

Reach out to your doctor if you are experiencing the following:

- Difficulty in urination
- Irregular heartbeat
- Numbness
- Tingling sensation
- Fainting

Rarely do the following occur but call in an emergency if you notice the following:

- Signs of liver issues such as like dark urine, yellowing of eyes and skin, stomach discomfort.
- Signs of stroke and heart attack.
- Decreased erection in men
- Allergies like itching, skin rashes, and the likes.

1.8.4.1 Precautions

Children should be closely monitored while on this drug, particularly for changes in mood. Furthermore, be sure to let your doctor know if you're:

- Hypersensitive to Atomoxetine or any of the components of the drug/
- If you are taking drugs in the MAOI class.

- If you have glaucoma, hyperthyroidism, high blood pressure, stroke symptoms, and the likes.
- If you are on other medications, so they rule out cases of drug-drug interaction.
- Atomoxetine can be drowsy. On the use of the drug, do not operate heavy machinery or drive.
- The drug can cause dizziness. So when you wake up, slowly stand up from the bed so you don't fall or faint.

Using the medicine may affect your ability to get a good night's sleep. Be sure to discuss any questions or concerns with your doctor or pharmacist. It is customary to take this medication in the morning split into many doses. You may have it either as a snack or as a meal.

1.8.5   Guanfacine

The drug is one of the medications used in treating ADHD, but it is not a first-line drug of choice. It can also be used to manage high blood pressure. The drug is not so preferred in the treatment of ADHD because of the extent of efficacy the previous drugs we discussed have shown.

It is an $\alpha_2\square$ adrenergic receptor agonist. This means that it works by activating the adrenergic receptors in the CNS, thereby regulating blood pressure and neurotransmitter levels in the CNS. It is also a Serotonin agonist.
Common side effects are:
- Dry mouth
- Dizziness
- Constipation
- Fatigue.

If any of these severe side effects occur, please see your doctor immediately:

- Serious dizziness
- Irregular heartbeat
- Mood changes can lead to suicidal thoughts.
- Allergic reactions like itching, rashes, and all.

1.8.6   Precautions

The drug should be used with caution in the following cases:

- If you are hypersensitive to guanfacine or any of the ingredients used in manufacturing.
- If you are pregnant or breastfeeding.
- If you are currently using other medications so they rule out a drug-drug interaction.
- If you have had a history of heart attack, stroke, and the likes.

It is of importance to note that the drug causes drowsiness, so do not operate machinery or drive while using the dose. The medication can be taken by mouth once daily with or without food and at bedtime.

1.9 Advantages of ADHD

Inattention, hyperactivity, and impulsivity are some the attention deficit hyperactivity disorder (ADHD). As with adults and adolescents, and children, it is believed that it may impact individuals of all ages. You've probably heard the phrase, "there is ability in disabilities." This phrase is true for ADHD patients, too. Many have been able to tweak the characteristics of ADHD to their advantage; this is possible through intentional practice, therapy, support from family and friends, and consultation of a social worker who has expertise in ADHD. This doesn't mean going for diagnosis and treatment is not needed. It means acknowledging that there is a problem or defining the problem, then using possible means to make the best out of life even with the neurodevelopmental dysfunction. The advantage of ADHD includes:

1. Ability to focus on what they are passionate about-Hyper focused. This can be seen in the way Mr. Wellington, an award-winning mural artist, rose to stardom. Originally, Mr. Wellington's life was debilitating because of the pressure from his family. He was born in an academic family. His mother had a Ph.D. in Economics and worked as a financial analyst for one of the leading media houses in the United States; similarly, his dad was a security consultant. He didn't perform well at school. He was reported to interrupt the class. If a pen should drop in the class, he becomes unexplainably curious, inattentive and generally, misses out on the subject of discourse. His grades went down the spiral. However, there was something that intrigued him greatly. It was painting, he made the highest score in their painting classes, but everyone seems to trivialize that. Nonetheless, his disruptive attitude was an issue in his vicinity, and this affected his interaction

with people as a bunch of his folks avoided him. When the Mom got a new job in Seattle, it was only thoughtful for them to have a change of environment for their son. The family relocated to Seattle, where the mom got a lecturing job at the State University. It was a new beginning for the family. Mrs. Tyler and Mr. Tyler (Wellington's parents) became more intentional about helping their son.

On their first visit to a social worker Dr. Caleb a buffed Mexican American who worked at the Medical school of the same University that Mrs. Tyler lectures. After going through Wellington's school report cards and essential information, Wellington was diagnosed with ADHD (Attention Deficit Hyperactivity Disorder). One thing stood out for Dr. Caleb. It was Wellington's high grade in his painting classes. Dr. Caleb enquired if the parent had done anything to boost Wellington's interest in painting, and they confessed to not have noticed it, talking more of supporting him. Wellington started his Psychotherapy and soon began to learn how to manage and organize himself. On one of Wellington's visits to the clinic, this time he went alone, he dabbled into a group of mural artists making magic in one of the walls in the children clinic, he stood there amazed, the artist noticed his interest and brought him closer. He missed his therapy session for that day as a result of his amazement. When Dr. Caleb found out why he missed the session. It became obvious to Dr. Caleb that Wellington was intrigued by painting. With the permission of the parent, Wellington was enrolled in a Mural Painting organization. Wellington had a great interest in his craft, hyper-focused, and made a lot of mouth-opening paintings. With his Impulsivity, he mixes a wide variety of colors, which turns out amazing and outstanding. During the exhibition of his creative art, the governor of the State purchased some of his paintings. Wellington's painting was sold across the United

States. Currently, he is using painting as a therapy for children and adults living with ADHD (Attention Deficit Hyperactivity Disorder). Hyperfocus is one of the features of ADHD. Because his family was intentional about helping him, they made him discover his strength which he is using to make an impact today.

2.   Creativity is one of the superpowers of people who have ADHD. They stay glued to things they are passionate about. This is a feature that even people without ADHD poses. However, people with ADHD can tweak, experiment, and revolutionize things in a way that's uncommon. They become attached to a particular task if they're passionate about it in a seemingly unhealthy way. Robin has already started building airplane prototypes, he did this from folding cartons with some slim steel for extensibility at a young age. He did things that his mate couldn't fathom. Even though his grades were not very appealing or enticing. He always thought outside the box. He loved doing practical things like picking cartons, dismantling them, and using some glue to put them together into a colorful house, something that an architect bought for some thousands of dollars as opposed to sitting down and following one pattern of learning daily. Young Robin was able to fix his dad's bad car tires once he had all the equipment required.

The ability of people with ADHD to think outside the box is best improved when they get a diagnosis from an expert that has a lot of experience working with ADHD patients, follow their training and coaching and medication if it doesn't have any side effects on them. For people like Robin, where normal people make mistakes and sob for weeks or probably stop trying. He didn't even notice he missed; he is very spontaneous and keeps putting things together until it becomes a masterpiece, and even after making such an awesome win, he doesn't celebrate for long. He looks out for the next unnoticed thing to amplify to greatness. These sets of people have a mind that, if carefully managed, turns their disabilities into something that appeals to all.

You've probably heard of Michael Phelps, one of the greatest Olympic swimmers of all time. Before retirement, he had a total of 28 medals and 23 gold medals. Phelps was diagnosed with ADHD at age 9. He was called dumb most of the time as a result of his poor performance in school. Most of his teachers had a low opinion of him. Some said he would never succeed. Today, he found his inner creativity in the pool, and against all difficulties posed by the dysfunction he has, he made it through. Today we know him for being able to exude creativity in the pool. Today he is a source of hope to people and a positive role model for people living with ADHD (Attention Deficit Hyperactivity Disorder).

3.   Most of the time, ADHD people come off as highly distracted, impulsive, and hyperactive. In fact, merely looking at their credit scores and academic records, you could be tempted to call them dumb. They are not dumb; some are genius that sees the world in an unpopular way. Their pattern of thinking and processing of information is what researchers call 'flexible thinking.' The flexible thinking helps ADHD individuals portray a high level of humor. Jasmine, a seventeen years old lady, was diagnosed with ADHD when she was 15 years old. Jasmine loved to talk; he often danced involuntarily in class, disrupting learning. She would stand up abruptly in class, then say something that will make his classmates burst into laughter. She made the classroom fun for a bunch of her mates, and her absence was always noticed

with uncharacterized quietness in class. The only issue was that she does this unsolicited. Her teacher observed her involvement in music and random shows in school and recommended to the parents that she join a dance and stand-up comedy group. In these two groups, Jasmine suddenly grew weary of dancing majorly because of how other members of that group perceived her. However, she focused on stand-up comedy. When she steps on the stage, grabs the mic, she fidgets and says a lot of unrelated stuff at a time, which is quite confusing and entertaining to her audiences. While she learned how to manage and organize herself. Her biggest issue was letting event managers believe she had the ability to entertain their guests, and whenever they permitted her, she left everyone happy and significantly confused.

She became irresistibly popular, and one of her ways of helping other people with related deficiency was by helping them discover the ability in their dysfunction. She now advocates to parents of ADHD children that their wards dysfunction can be managed and that it is not the end of life for anyone with ADHD.

4.   Funny as it may sound, you get to surprise yourself a couple of times. For instance, Mr. Edwin, a twenty-three years old saxophonist, seems never to stop surprising himself. He always found some dollar bills in his pocket. He always forgot he had money somewhere, and whenever he dabbles into this, he is so pleased and radiates a beaming smile. This is not to say forgetfulness is an advantage of ADHD, but to emphasize that this characteristic could be a pleasure mechanism. Imagine being broke and not knowing you have some money nearby, then suddenly you found this money in a cloth you wanted to launder, how would you feel?

5.   Energy is one of the superpowers of ADHD patients. They possess a lot of energy, which in the beginning phase of the manifestation of the dysfunction is usually termed disruptive. Again, this energy can be harnessed into useful potentials that would benefit the world at large. The case of Lewis is not different. Lewis was diagnosed of ADHD (Attention Deficit Hyperactivity Disorder); he often ran around the compound playing with anything he could lift. He almost ran into a moving vehicle across the street, thanks to an observant pedestrian who helped save his life. Before his diagnosis, his parents were not well informed about the dysfunction, therefore, this made them sad. They thought it was over for their children. They almost gave up on their child as result of the report that came in. Frequently, Lewis's teachers and principal would call in complaining of Lewis's behavior. This affected the parent greatly, especially the dad. It was on a Sunday morning that Lewis ran up the alter when the Presiding pastor was preaching. The church didn't really get disturbed because everyone thought it was a childhood thing. The church usher had to take Lewis out of the congregation to at least keep Lewis's parent focused on the sermon.

After service, when Lewis's parents went to pick him up, it was the usher that suggested they see a social worker. The usher suspected that he had ADHD. That was the family's first time hearing it. The parents heeded to the usher's advice and went to see a clinical psychologist called Dr. Carlos, an African American expert in ADHD within their neighborhood. On reaching Dr. Carlos's office, some 2.5 km journey from their home. Dr. Carlos received them warmly and requested for a detailed history of Lewis's life and activities in school. After some professional work performed on the information provided by the parent, Lewis was diagnosed with ADHD. This brought sorrow to the family, however, Dr. Carlos' explanation of possible options gave them something to hope on. Immediately, Lewis was signed up for coaching and soon he began to learn conscious control of himself and began to take the prescribed medication for ADHD. His interest in tracks and Fields heightened the day Dr. Carlos invited him over for dinner. After the sumptuous meal served by Dr. Carlos' wife. He showed him around including all he achieved in his teenage age in track and field. The curiosity he showed was appealing to Dr. Carlos. Lewis soon joined a track and field team that Dr. Carlos suggested. He didn't perform well in the long-distance race, however, he was excellent in splinting. His Fame went abroad like a wildfire; when he represented the country in Rio 2016 and got the gold medal for his speed. He is widely celebrated in the country and abroad for his giant stride. His energy was channeled into something he loves, and today he is a role model to people living with ADHD.

In conclusion, everyone can be great through thoughtful and intention practice of one's gift, however, the brain of an attention deficit hyperactivity disorder patient is differently wired from the brain of a normal individual. This proffers more energy than that of a normal Child. This energy, when discovered, can be harnessed into a powerful weapon for change. Michael Phelps, a pro swimmer, conquered his fears and that of his teachers, who thought he would not amount to anything. He was intrigued by swimming and then channeled his energy into it and became the best in his time. Today he is a beacon of hope to everyone, whether you're living with ADHD or not.

2 UNDERSTANDING YOUR CHILD'S CONDITION

2.1 Facts on the Child Brain Development

Researchers are still learning about ADHD, as well as brain development. There are so many indications that suggest that the differences in some components of the brain are part of what makes it much harder for people with ADHD to concentrate and maintain focus, especially when they are not interested in it.

ADHD is a neurodevelopmental disorder, which implies that there are some deficits that can alter the normal development of a child's brain. However, this does not necessarily mean a negative impact on intelligence. The main effect of this deficit is an inability to regulate emotions and attention, thereby resulting in hyperactivity and impulsivity. Some may also experience problems with organization.

2.1.1   Normal Brain Explained

For more than 20 years now, different studies have emerged to show that about 95% of the total brain volume of a young adult is achieved at age 5 to 7. Also, research shows that the total cerebral volume (TCV) reaches maximum before adolescence.

A study involving 45 kids between age 5 and 11, of which MRI scans were taken at two years intervals, revealed a noticeable expansion of the brian by 1 mm yearly. This expansion was majorly at the prefrontal cortex. Upon cross-sectional analyses, an age-related ventricular increase in the size of the TCV and a corresponding decrease in the lenticular nucleus and the thalamus.

Studies have also identified that the cerebellum and the cerebrum are generally larger in boys than in girls. This is the main reason why the cortical gray matter is also larger in boys than in girls. Other features that are larger in boys include the subcortical regions, the globus pallidus, and the putamen. The only feature that is larger in girls is caudate.

2.1.1.1   White and gray matter development

Longitudinal and cross-sectional analyses of the brain have shown a consistent increase in the volume of white matter within the pediatric age range. This increase was greater in the male gender, and a corresponding increase n myelination is observed within the same age range.

In a cross-sectional study performed using 110 adolescents and children between the ages of 4 to 17, the age-related changes in the neural tracts were examined. An increase in the white matter of the posterior portion and internal capsule of the left arcuate fasciculus was identified. White matter development was also seen in specific regions like the corpus callosum, where the increase was first identified, followed by a posterior growth during adolescence.

The growth of gray matter follows a more heterogeneous pattern. In general, the gray matter decreases from childhood through to post-adolescence. However, the decrease does not follow a linear fashion. The general progression is a 13% increase and growth in the gray matter between age 6 to 9, followed by a 5% decrease every decade.

2.1.2   ADHD Brain Explained

There are so many questions that surround ADHD. Some people still ask if the condition is real or simply a lack of willpower, bad parenting, or lack of motivation. None of these is true, and such comments will only make you feel vulnerable, especially if you have a child with ADHD.

One of the major things you should know is that there are several biological differences in the brain of a normal person and that of a person with ADHD. These differences can be divided into three areas: function, structure, and chemistry.

2.1.2.1 Brain Function

Until a few decades ago, there was a general lack of understanding of how the brain worked, but advancements in brain imaging today make it feasible to comprehend how the brain works fully. Use of the following techniques include:

- Functional magnetic resonance imaging (fMRI)
- Single-photon emission computer tomography (SPECT)
- Positron emission tomography (PET)

ADHD research showed that some brain regions had different blood flow levels in people with the disease compared to those who didn't have it. Additionally, reduced blood flow to the prefrontal areas has also been found. In general, a reduction in the flow of blood to the brain can ultimately decrease the activity of the brain.

The prefrontal region of the brain is the main house for different executive functions. It is the part that is responsible for tasks, including organizing, remembering, emotional reactions, paying attention, and planning.

Research data suggests a relationship between ADHD and brain dysfunction. MRI suggests that people with ADHD usually have higher functional connectivity in some parts of the brain compared to other parts.

2.1.2.2 Brain Structure

Research work has also revealed an obvious structural difference between a normal brain and an ADHD brain. People with ADHD usually have lesser brain volume, especially in five subcortical areas. This brings about an ultimate reduction in the size of their brain, and the difference is more in children than in adults.

In individuals with ADHD, the brain is never completely developed. In addition, the hippocampus and amygdala are smaller among those with ADHD, which is also intriguing. These two regions of the brain play an essential part in impulsiveness and emotional treatment.

2.1.2.3 Brain Chemistry

The brain is characterized by different communication networks, all of which are implicated in the transfer of messages and information between brain cells (neurons). The gap between these neurons is known as a synapse. Before a message can be transported from one neuron to another, these synapses must be filled with chemical messengers called neurotransmitters.

There are different types of neurotransmitters, and they all have different functions they perform. In ADHD, noradrenaline and dopamine are the key neurotransmitters. The dopamine system is dysregulated in an ADHD brain, unlike in a normal brain. An ADHD brain will either underutilize dopamine or lack sufficient receptors or even the neurotransmitter itself.

2.1.3   Neuroimaging Patterns Predict ADHD Symptoms

Demographic and behavioral data, alongside MRI scans showing brain patterns, have helped in predicting some of the symptoms of ADHD in both children and even some adults. Evidence of this finding can be seen in the American Journal of Psychiatry, in which different researchers carried out an in-depth examination on MRI scans of about 160 Australian kids. These kids were between 9 and 12 years of age. Four pervasive brain profiles were identified, and this was indicative of certain ADHD symptoms.

Advanced MRI modeling was used in documenting brain changes from different viewpoints. The aim was to identify common patterns through different anatomical scales that can be related to cognitive abilities or ADHD symptoms. The results obtained from this study suggest that some of the unique symptoms that are experienced by children with ADHD can be related to the biology of the brain.

About 70 of the children in this study were diagnosed with ADHD, and up to 25 were receiving medications to help them manage the condition. During this study, different assessment strategies were employed, and the aim was to track demographic characteristics and symptoms. The assessments span for 4 hours, and they included a self-reported survey, parent questionnaire, and cognitive evaluation.

A combination of MRI scans, psychographic data, demographic data, and assessments made it possible for researchers to identify four different brain patterns. These patterns can be associated with demographic and behavioral profiles for application in predicting symptoms of ADHD in different groups of children.

1. **Development:** Children that are less developmentally mature have a higher tendency to become hyperactive. Such kids will need to receive medication for ADHD. Also, younger brain age is a common thing with ADHD children, especially those who are less developmentally mature.

2. **Cognitive Performance:** The identified patterns were also related to reduced cognitive performance, few hyperactivity symptoms, and higher irritability which is not associated with ADHD. Certain environment components were also identified. This includes maternal smoking, poor quality of life, and low parental education,

3. **Male Hyperactivity:** The profiles of children under this category suggest that the male child has a higher tendency to become hyperactive, and this was further included from different rating scales of teachers and parents. Also, such kids tend to have a higher likelihood of comorbidities and other social problems. Pre-pubescent male children are more likely to experience these changes.

4. **Size of the Head:** While boys' and girls' academic achievement is related to their brain size, boys have a much greater brain capacity than girls. This is because academic performance, cognitive ability, and brain size are all interrelated.

More studies are done regularly, and the aim is to have a better and more advanced neurological understanding of ADHD.

2.1.4   Brain Maturation Delayed, Not Deviant, in ADHD Children

Similar to what was said before, children with ADHD have a more difficult time with brain growth, especially with cortical development. People prone to being distracted have a more significant impact on their attention and working memory, with the prefrontal lobe as the most impacted portion of the brain.

There's currently a debate on whether the delay in the development of the brain is a cause of ADHD. Some are of the opinion that ADHD can be associated with the deviation of normal brain development.

There are different researches that have been performed to help resolve this controversy. One such research was performed by Philip Shaw and this was a neuroanatomical study. The results of this research associated ADHD with a delay in brain maturation rather than a deviation in cortical maturation.

In Shaw's research, the thickness of the cortex was measured in about 450 kids, half of which were normal, and the other half with ADHD. Scans of the brain of these kids were taken twice, over a three-year interval. Also, the participants in this research included young adults and preschoolers between 7 and 16 years. 92% of the kids with ADHD had the combined type of ADHD.

The cortical thickness was estimated from over 800 MRI scans and the focus was on finding the age at which the cortical thickness got to its peak. In general, kids without ADHD got to their peak cortical thickness at age 8, which those with ADHD didn't get to peak cortical thickness until age 10.

The study also revealed that the delay in the cortical natural was more evident in the lateral prefrontal cortex, which is a supportive feature for cognitive functions like executive attention control, suppressing inappropriate thoughts and responses, working memory, and evaluating reward contingencies. The primary motor cortex is the only area of the brain in which children with ADHD experience early maturation.

2.1.4.1 What is responsible for the delay?

According to Shaw and his team of researchers, genetic factors and psychostimulants had a major role to play. Psychostimulants are implicated because most of the participants in the study were on one psychostimulant or the other. The research team also suggested that the psychostimulants had trophic effects in the ADHD group. Even if the psychostimulants' impact on grey matter volume was not detected, this is still possible. Therefore, no one can argue that genetics was not a significant influence.

2.2 First Diagnosis

Inattentiveness, hyperactivity, and impulsivity are all characteristics of an attention deficit disorder (ADHD). CDC reports that eleven percent of U.S. youngsters have ADHD. This neurodevelopmental condition is diagnosed based on observed symptoms in children and adults. The DSM-5 includes a checklist of signs that a doctor must check to conclude that a kid has ADHD. These criteria are classified according to the types of ADHD the child has.

For sixteen years and below, the child is expected to have at least six of the nine symptoms in one or both types of ADHD. Adolescents seventeen and above, on the other hand, must exhibit five of the nine symptoms of both kinds of ADHD in order to get their diagnosis. Attention Deficit Hyperactivity Disorder has three primary characteristics: inattention, hyperactivity, and impulsivity. When parents or guardian of a child gets notified of this diagnosis, these pieces of information often inundate them. Many other disorders could manifest the symptoms of ADHD, for example, anxiety, depression, sleep disorder, and learning disabilities. It's important that the evaluator does not confuse the symptoms of the above-mentioned neural disorders for ADHD. This chapter hopes to explore what should be done after the child's diagnosis has been reported.

Firstly, as a parent or a guardian of the child, it's normal to be emotional about what your ward is going through. However, it's in the best interest of the ward, yourself (the parent), and the community that you (the parents) accept the diagnosis. Acknowledgment of the diagnosis is important so that assistance that's due to the child can commence immediately. Knowing and accepting that there is a challenge that problem-solving strategies can be employed or deployed. If you're in doubt of the diagnosis, consult another center with expertise in the diagnosis and management of ADHD as soon as possible so that the behavior of your child doesn't deteriorate.

Now that you must have accepted the diagnosis, it's important you become informed on what ADHD is. This requires conscious or intentional study of relevant articles on ADHD. You have to understand the basics of ADHD, symptoms, different medications pattern, differential diagnoses, Psychotherapy, and all the relevant information that would be useful to your child's management and recovery. Another way to get information about ADHD is by having a session with an ADHD, brain development, and children educator expert. This is usually a Neuropsychologist or social worker with expertise in ADHD. He or she would best explain how the brain works in normal and pathologic conditions like that of ADHD. Again, it's important that you have complete knowledge of neurodevelopmental dysfunction like ADHD; other people who relate with the child should also understand what ADHD means. This will help Foster support for the child both at home and in school. Examples of such persons are the teachers, friends, siblings, and relatives who constantly visit your home.

Why is it important that you divulge your ward's diagnosis to the teacher?

It's because the teacher acts as the child's parent in school when you are away. Some the strategies that should be employed by the teacher and school management as proposed by experts are extended time giving to the child on assignment and tests, the child should be brought close to the teacher to avoid fidgeting, and this makes the child easily accessible to the ward should there be an emergency. Also, the use of graphs and chat is greatly encouraged. All this mechanism is to ensure that the child feels supported and understood.

Now that you've sensitized the siblings, the class teacher, the school management, and other relatives frequently visit you about your child's challenges if he or she has one. It's now important you sensitize your ward about his or her diagnosis; this would help him interrupt some of the stimulus he receives, like the urge to shout abruptly in class or make funny gestures that disrupt learning. This is particularly difficult as there may be an outburst of emotions between both parties (the parents and the child). However, some talking points could work as suggested by experts;

- Tell the child all there is about ADHD, the symptoms, the medications, to mention but a few.
- Make him or her understand that he or she has a brain, a special one indeed. This could be done by letting him know that he has a type of brain that thinks fast and simultaneously, and this could be distracting as he or she has many ideas at the same time.
- Let the child know that his diagnosis is not a death sentence.
- Make the child feel and know that he is not the only one with the neurodevelopmental dysfunction. Show them statistics of people in the United States of America who have ADHD if you live in the US. If you don't, show him or her statistics of people in your country that have been diagnosed with ADHD. Again, it's also smart to show him celebrities that had or have ADHD. Celebrities like Michael Phelps, an Olympic champion

in swimming; Simone Biles, a US Olympic champion in gymnastics, Justin Timberlake, a Grammy-winning singer and actor, Adam Levine, a singer, Ty Pennington, a TV home repair guru, Terry Bradshow, a super bowl champion to mention but a few. Making these known to him will give him reasons to believe in himself amidst the dysfunction and a sense of belonging. These would also be a source of motivation for him or her. Again, this will show the child role possible role models to choose from.

- Inform the child about the recovery mechanism you intend to deploy and always inform him or her when there is a change in the intended strategy. If your child is going to be taking medications, don't castigate the drugs. This gives the child something to look forward to. This strategy makes the child feel carried along

Now that you have earned the trust of your ward, it's best to look out for treatment plans. The treatment plan could be pharmacological intervention or nonpharmacological intervention. The pharmacological intervention involves the use of stimulants and nonstimulants. ADHD affects the prefrontal cortex that carries out executive function, making it difficult for the child to follow through on tasks. Again, ADHD is usually associated with reduced dopamine. Stimulants are drugs that work on dopamine, a neurotransmitter that modulates the reward pathways. The stimulants can be long-lasting, which means it's potent for twelve to sixteen hours and more, and the short-acting ones last for three to six hours.

Examples of long-acting drugs are Dextroamphetamine (Adderall XR), Dexmethylphenidate (Focalin XR),

Lisdexamfetamine (Vyvanse), and Methylphenidate. Therefore, there may be a need to take the stimulants multiple times a day. Research has shown that pharmacological intervention is essential in mitigating the effect of ADHD symptoms. These drugs help to improve ADHD symptoms. According to a study published by Lancet psychiatry, it states that it's "the easiest to tolerate and most effective option for an adolescent is methylphenidate (With a brand name as Ritalin, Concerta, Daytrana, Aptensio XR, Metadate CD, and Methylin to mention a few.)". Research suggests that using a drug as an intervention doesn't work twenty percent of the time. However, it has been shown to be eighty percent effective. Parents or guardians are frequently concerned about the risk of addiction or abuse of drugs. However, researchers suggest that it's better to offer the child stimulants than, leaving him to find one for himself. This is the common cause of substance abuse amongst ADHD patients. The parent should oversee the administration of the drugs to their child or wards to prevent substance abuse.

Another commonly-raised worry by parents of patients with ADHD is that they are concerned about side effects from the medications. Recently, the Food and Drug Administration (FDA) authorized a medication that may be given throughout the night, and its effect is seen the following morning. This helps in giving the child an easy start for the morning. The name of this drug is Methylphenidate Hypochloride. This drug is available to both adults and children with ADHD. The drug mentioned above could be effective and may elicit side effects. For adults, it may cause weight loss as the stimulant or drug reduces appetite, while for children, it can lead to stunted growth. To mitigate these side effects, the parents or caregivers should be proactive in providing the adult or children with a healthy and balanced diet before taking their medications. The potential adverse effects include faster heart rate, higher blood pressure, and difficulty sleeping. It is also possible that one's personality may alter.

According to Dr. Hallowell, stimulants are the golden standard. However, in some cases where it doesn't work as it should, nonstimulant medication could be used. Nonstimulant increases the activities of the neurotransmitters that regulate attention. This neurotransmitter is called norepinephrine. This nonstimulant acts in short, intermediate, and long terms like stimulant drugs. The notable side effects of nonstimulant are their ability to sedate a child and decrease blood pressure.

They are treatment plans without medications in the management of ADHD patients. This is frequently called occupational therapy or nonpharmacological interventions for people with ADHD. Occupational therapy helps moderate the interaction between the child's environment and the Brain. It helps the child manage his or her won reflexes. Also, doing sporting activities could help the ADHD patient manage himself well. During sporting activities, the ward or child learns how to control him or herself, reduces Impulsivity, and the field becomes an outlet for him to express him or herself energetically. Examples of such sports are horseback riding, soccer, swimming, and wall climbing, to mention but a few. Sporting activities elevate the level of neurotransmitters in the brain.

Music therapy is a big way to attend to an ADHD patient. Music itself is soothing to the brain and relaxes the brain. This therapy stimulates the happy hormones that mediate memories and concentration. Also playing Musical Instruments can be helpful too. It plays the same role as when someone plays the instrument for you. Also, arts such as painting, dancing, yoga, singing could play a role in stimulating the rewards pathways, which helps relax the patient as well.

In conclusion, ADHD can be managed even though thirty percent of people that were diagnosed in childhood continue with it to adulthood. However, this fit comes with intentional practice, which may be overwhelming. It's important that you accept your fate or your child's fate. Carry out a complete study of the neurodevelopmental dysfunction as this could be done by reading up academic articles on the subjects that are often available online or reaching out to a neuropsychologist for complete information on the dysfunction. This will help you make informed decisions as they arise. Again, the child, the neuropsychologist, or a social worker with expertise in ADHD, the child's teacher if he or she is in school, is important for evaluating and managing ADHD. This set of people will be a form of support for the child both at home and in his or her school. Informing the child about his diagnosis would really make him aware that interruptive mechanisms can be brought to play when symptoms start to manifest. The child deserves support from his school and parents regardless of his dysfunction. Hence, he should be carried along because this makes him trust the regimens that may be employed in the future.

2.3   Accepting your Child's ADHD

A child with ADHD can still live a normal, happy, and a fulfilled life. As a parent, you owe it to yourself and your child to ensure that child lives life to the fullest. The first step to ensuring a child with ADHD lives normally is to come to terms and accept the fact that your child has ADHD. With acceptance comes the recognition and the need for management and self-care.

As parents, you should ensure that your child gets the best medical care. Also, we should be very careful about the kind of things we say to the child. Always ensure that the child is not left out among other children.

The purpose of this chapter is to discuss the importance of accepting your child's ADHD, what you as a parent should not say to a child with ADHD, and general care and parenting tips for handling children with ADHD.

Managing ADHD can be done through medication, education, counseling, and therapy. Also, as a parent, there are a couple of things you should and should not do. Let's discuss them.

2.3.1   Parenting Hacks For Children With ADHD.

As a parent, you need to take in different approaches and methods as coping mechanisms to deal with a child who has ADHD. It can get difficult and frustrating sometimes, especially when the child becomes aggressive or hyper.

ADHD presents differently in youngsters. Concerning your kid, there are a variety of ways in which ADHD will impact him. However, in general, ADHD can affect children in the following ways:

1. Some children show signs of being easily distracted. So they tend not to listen, easily forget instructions, hardly pay attention, always need reminders for tasks, and do not seem to put in effort in school work.

2. In some children, they start being hyperactive. Then they become disorganized and messy, they can't sit still, they rush things, and they make careless mistakes.

3. In other children, they start to become impulsive. They start to butt into conversations and activities a lot, they start to become aggressive, imbibe a lack of control. They have trouble being patient or with sharing. They start to do things without thinking and even do things they should not do.

As a parent, it is normal to confuse these actions of your children as normal and see them as having a phase. But when your child has been diagnosed with ADHD, here are things you can do to help them improve.

- **Take an active role in their treatment**: Decide to be active in your child's treatment. Ensure they don't skip their appointment dates. Ask necessary questions. Ensure your child takes their medications as prescribed. Do not change doses of the medications. Ensure their medicines are kept safe. Also, read up on ADHD and gather as much information as possible that might help your child.

- ADHD varies in different children, so as a parent, you have to know how the symptoms of ADHD manifests in your child. Whether it is the Distracted stage, or the Hyperactive stage, or Impulsive stage, each stage has its own symptoms that a child would manifest. As a parent, study your child to know the symptoms he or she exhibits, and ask questions from your therapist on the best approach for the child. For example, some children have issues with attention, so you know how to give best practices that help the child to focus.

- **Set SMART Goals and Expectations**: As a parent, it is very important to set goals and manage your expectations. This comes from tackling one problem at a time. Rather than trying to tackle attention, impulsiveness, and hyperactivity at once, pick one of them at a time and tackle it with the right approach, and when you see considerable improvements, you can move on to the next one.

- **Create Structure**: Ensure you teach your child healthy habits. They might be slow in responding to corrections, but it would be worth it in the end. Make sure to give them routines like them arranging their uniforms before school the next day. Give them tasks that are easy to carry out and easy to do for each activity, like eating, bedtime, etc.

- Ensure you make your child feel loved. Build their self-esteem, and reward them when they do things right. It would help motivate them to want to be better. Be patient with your child and ensure that their medications are taken right. Also, protect them from unfavorable and harmful environments. Environments that would affect their self-esteem and make them more aware of their condition.

- As a parent, you should liaise with your child's teacher in school to create a favorable and conducive learning environment. We know that children with ADHD would not learn at the same pace as their peers. While it is not advisable to separate them from their peers, ensure the teacher creates a conducive atmosphere where your child will be free to express him/herself and learn at their pace. If possible, educate your child's teacher on the condition.

- Spend quality time with your child. Never make your child feel like having ADHD is their fault. Ensure you play with them, take them out to parks, watch them do what they love, cheer them on.

- As a parent raising a child with ADHD can be overwhelming; take time out for yourself. Protect your mental health, so you don't end up lashing out at the child. Do the things you love doing to keep your mind sane and your body healthy.

Other things you can do as a parent raising a child with ADHD include:

- Limit distractions. Things that will easily distract the childlike televisions, video games, playtime, should be limited so as to train the child on focus.

- Engage in exercise regularly. When your child exercises regularly, it trains the child on how to focus on a specific task and may decrease the activity of impulsiveness. Also, it helps stimulate the child's brain.

- Regulate sleep pattern. Helps the child relax and become used to routine activities.

- Encourage the child to speak up. This helps the child to talk about feelings and prevent resentment. Also builds the child's self-esteem.

- Believe in your child's ability to promote confidence.

- Teach patience. This helps them to think before they act or talk.

- Take care of yourself as a Parent.

Here are things you should not DO as a Parent raising a child with ADHD. They are:

- Make compromises sometimes. Not every time be rigid, sometimes be flexible with your child's routines and learning. When he or she completes most of their assigned tasks, reward them. This serves as a form of encouragement for them to do better next time.

- Do not be negative. The truth is that most times, feelings often translate into actions. So if you have a negative mindset towards your child, you won't know when you would start to act it out. This would affect your child negatively and improve the condition.

- Do not become too frustrated and overwhelmed. As a parent raising a child with the condition, we understand the feeling of overwhelm and frustrations you might have. But don't let it get to you. Protect your mind, thoughts, and actions. Do things that would keep you sane.

- Do not forget to give your child their medication or to skip their therapy sessions. This is very important.

Things You Should Not Say To A Child With ADHD

1. Nobody needs to know you have ADHD. This might make your child feel alone. Then he would start to stay on his own more. Instead, tell them not to keep their condition a secret. Telling people helps a lot.

2. ADHD will stop when you are older. This will build lots of expectations and make the child live in false pretense. Telling them the truth early enough would help them accept their conditions, want to get help, want to do better, and move on to become the best versions of themselves.

3. Having ADHD is Not an Excuse. Your child doing things differently is not his or her fault. Their behavior is way different from a normal child. So when finding out why they misbehaved, ask what happened.

In summary, raising a child with ADHD can be tasking as they require special attention. Here are few ways to show them, love:

1. Learn to separate the child's personality from their behavior at that point. It helps make them feel loved.

2. Keep a cool tone with them.

3. Keep consistent rules.

4. Keep your emotions under check always.

5. Do one thing at a time for them to emulate.

6. Give your child tasks to carry out. This helps build responsibility.

7. Remember the names and dosages of each medication your child is taking and give them regularly.

8. Keep the medication away from their reach to avoid them misusing it.

9. Do not overindulge your child.

10.   Keep your child's therapist updated always.

Here are ways you can show a form of discipline without frightening your child:

1. Give rewards every time your child completes his or her task.

2. Give them praises.

3. Ignore really minor behaviors.

4. Give clear and effective instructions.

In the management of ADHD in children, the therapist advises that you use the two principles of behavior management therapy. These principles are:

1. Use of reward systems.

2. Use of punishment, like depriving them of their favorite if they don't get a task done.

As a parent raising a child with ADHD, we really hope this chapter helps you realize that they can still lead normal lives.

Only if you practice the strategies here and the ones from your therapist, also remember to take time out for yourself and protect your mental health as well.

2.4 Strategies for managing a child with ADHD.

People with Attention Deficit Hyperactivity Disorder (a neurodevelopmental dysfunction) exhibit inattentiveness, Impulsivity, and hyperactivity as a part of their behavioral pattern. Childrearing is a wholesome and tedious task; however, raising an ADHD child is even more difficult and demanding. They have a functionally different brain with reduced functionality of the prefrontal cortex that coordinates executive functions like learning, motivation, and coordination. The parent, social worker, pediatrician, school teacher, and school management must be informed of the child's diagnosis. This would increase the attention, resources, and support the child receives. Empathy is the key to managing ADHD children or adults. Empathy has to do with genuinely understanding how the child feels and responding to him as meekly as possible. This is vital because children with ADHD don't know or understand the level of disruption they cause in school or at home, so being empathetic is essential in dealing with ADHD children. How do you cope and manage a child with hyperactivity, inattentiveness, and that acts out of impulse? This chapter explores the strategies for managing such a child.

First, be calm; you're not alone. As a parent, it's truly overwhelming to have a child manifesting the symptoms of ADHD. It implies multiple and intentional activities. It's practically impossible to help your child when you're not calm. Children learn from looking and observing things around them. Now, how do you help a Hyperactive child when you, as the parent, are frustrated and even aggravated, too. There are about seventeen million people with ADHD in the United

States. So be at ease because you're not alone. Again, being calm ensures trust, and when the child can trust you, they will most probably be able to heed whatever instructions you offer them. Acknowledging that your ward or child has ADHD is the first step to calmness; if you're genuinely interested in your child's welfare. You need healthy mental health to deal with a ward or child that has Attention Deficit Hyperactivity Disorder. The possible way to do this is by taking breaks intermittently, such as but not limited to taking a walk in the park, going to the gym, go grab some food in the restaurant, and cold water bath. Therefore, you need someone to serve as an assistant, such as a nanny that is also informed of the child diagnosis and that would take care of your child why you refuel during the break period. Being calm gives you more time to make an informed decision that will help the child greatly. Don't give up on your child; he or she deserves all the attention you can afford. Being calm would mean you must not yell at your child as this would exacerbate his situation, therefore, ruin the goal of helping him organize himself.

Establish a flexible rule of conduct and instructions that the child should follow. First, define what these principles are, and it should be targeted at helping the child coordinate his or her activities, like creating a time for a meal, a time to sleep, a time to study and do assignments, a time to exercise. Being flexible is being aware that the child would make mistakes as he is not a robot. It's pertinent that you exercise Patience and Love towards your child. As the child has disabilities in coordinating himself; therefore, acting out of impulse. It's imperative that you help him coordinate things. In establishing a flexible rule of conduct, ensure that there is a reward for some activities carried out. The reward is to help the child aspire to something or look forward to more rewards, thereby leading to a tweak in destructive behaviors.

However, there should be punishment for every task that wasn't carried out. Punishment refers to the "cost for the child's choice." In giving rewards or punishment, ensure you're consistent because inconsistency would do more harm than good in the child's general response to your rule of conduct. Also, activities should be time-regulated. Lack of sleep would heighten the child's risk of inattention, hyperactivity, and Impulsivity, and you don't want that. So measures should be put in place to help the child get adequate sleep. Again, to aid the child catch a sufficient amount of sleep, avoid meals with a high amount of sugar and caffeine as they inhibit sleeping mechanisms. For receptivity, experts advise you make a list of the rule of conduct visible to the child. This can be done by putting the rules on the wall. This helps the child know what to do and what not to do. Establish what the child should or shouldn't do when in a clash with his peers, either to walk away or inform the teacher about what has happened.

Nonetheless, there should be a framework on which every rule runs on. This means that the rule of conduct should be structured so that it's straightforward and unambiguous, which would facilitate integration and understanding. If the child doesn't understand any of the tasks, do well to explain to him or her positively.

Provide room to exercise. Exercises give them an avenue to exact their enormous amount of energy. It helps them focus on specific movements to truly enjoy the sport, which in the long run aids coordination. Experts say that sports reduce depression, anxiety, and Impulsivity. The exercising moment should be time-framed. Good exercises enhance sleep, which would be essential when they wake up. Exercise helps excite neurotransmitters like dopamine that children with ADHD are short on, which then reduces Impulsivity. Examples of sport for ADHD are running, climbing, gymnastics, karate, yoga, skating, to mention a few. These exercises impact positively on executive function.

Chores should be broken down into small and manageable chunks. This is because they would be unable to focus when the task is too large. Extended time should be given to them to complete a task; this is to make up for every form of inattentiveness. Monitor them appropriately and always be positive and empathetic. ADHD behavior is often frustrating; try as much as possible to take a walk when you feel frustrated. This is better than trying to scold them.

Seek helps from teachers and school management if the child is of school age. When you're away, they're left with the teacher to deal with. That means the child needs extra resources than other pupils or Students. What can a teacher do to help your child's situation? The teacher should first be informed about his diagnosis, this would make him or her be proactive and intentional about helping the child. The teacher should help reduce distractions around him by not positioning the child close to the window or door as this would be more distracting for him because of people loitering around or items flying around and would distract the child greatly. Also, the child should not be kept close to his talkative classmates. At some point, the teacher should allow the child to walk rather than allow the child to sit in a single position. This is particularly difficult for hyperactivity and Impulsivity type of ADHD. Again, more time should be given to him or her on assignments and tests. This would cover up for delays due to inattentiveness. The teacher should have a fidget item nearby. Fidget tools such as tangle Jr, palm weight, monkey ring, these fidget toys help a great deal to reduce stress. It also provides an avenue for them to dispense their energy in a confined place without disturbing the tranquility of the community. The teacher should also incorporate the use of a planner. Planners help to keep the child organized and focused. It also shows him what he should be doing and not doing. Also, the use of a flowchart would be helpful, as it demonstrated a stepwise method of carrying out an array of activities. The child should be taught how to follow these tasks one step at a time. The teacher should incorporate breaks for the child to help him relax and prepare for the next task. Classwork should be broken down into small pieces where it's easy for the child to follow, and wherever there is a mistake, correct with patience and love. These activities may be overwhelming for the teacher since he or she has more than one child to manage. However, the teacher should try his or her best to optimize activities that Foster and improves the child's symptoms. The teacher should work with the school's guidance counselor and coach to help modulate the child's behavior.

Help your child eat well. Establish what they eat, when they eat, and the quantity they eat. Children with Impulsivity miss meals a lot; therefore, adequate supervision should be provided. An inadequate meal can deteriorate a normal child's physical, mental and emotional health. This is even worse for ADHD children because they may start looking out for other means to satisfy their hunger without reasoning the aftermath. Fatty and sugary foods should be deleted from the child's menu. Sugar and caffeine are unhealthy for children with ADHD because they lead to decreased sleep. Decreased sleep then lead to inattention. A trait we are trying to mitigate. ADHD children's meals should be rich in minerals and vitamins. Discuss with your pediatrician for more meals available and suitable for ADHD children.

Aid your child to create social skills. Children with ADHD often come off as absurd and aggressive; their behaviors are observed as oblivious because of how they act on impulse. They interrupt discussions and may call out in class. This trait makes befriending people with ADHD difficult. However, making friends is still possible by subtly and sincerely speaking to them about the difficulties surrounding their dysfunctions. Allow them to share their thoughts and challenges with you, and be prompt to correct them when they're becoming rude in their speech or communication. Make time for them to play with other children of his or her age. This can be achieved by taking them to a funfair, monitoring their interaction with other kids, note how other kids react to him or her, and make an informed decision with that; when you observe a positive behavior, do well to reward it. Teach him some social cues, make him understand that certain facial expressions indicate a certain mood. Show him or her the social cue that indicates; I want to talk to you and the one that doesn't. Show him to raise his or her hand when he or she has a concern in class or any social gatherings.

Decrease and regulate Television time. Children with ADHD hate to be idle as a result of their inherent hyperactivity. So they should be kept busy and allowed to do what intrigues them under surveillance from the parent or any caregiver. They could assist you in making meals. They could have fun-filled board games with their siblings if they have any. They could also take a hand on a lesson, which has been broken down to facilitate easy learning.

Incorporate art into their regular life. You can see to it that their room designed with beautiful art paintings. This will help them stay calm as those carefully painted art soothes the brain, increasing the production of the neurotransmitters lacking in

ADHD. These neurotransmitters would help excite the prefrontal lobe of the brain that coordinates executive functions in the human body.

In summary, don't give up on your child; he or she deserves all the care and love you can offer. Again always have it in mind that his behaviors are not willful; it results from a neurodevelopmental dysfunction. Managing an ADHD child amongst other parental responsibilities is tedious. The backbone of managing an ADHD child is empathy. Be empathetic and don't speak negatively to your child as this exacerbates his condition. There is help available at school, online for ADHD-related concerns. As a parent taking care of an ADHD child, remember to take care of yourself because it's only when you're sound physically and mentally that you would be able to care for your children and family.

2.5 How to improve your behavior toward your child with ADHD

Hyperactivity, inattentiveness, and Impulsivity are the common characteristics of ADHD. Children with ADHD exhibit either or all of the above-mentioned common characteristics. It affects people of all ages. It's commonly diagnosed by evaluating the child's behavior and comparing such behavior to a normal Child of his chronological age. For adults, it can be diagnosed by looking at the person's education, financial, and relationship history. This behavior often causes unrest in school, home, and social gatherings if it's not tamed. The responsibility of taming this inattentive, Hyperactive and impulsive behavior falls heavily on the shoulder of the child's parent. However, the child's school teacher, school management, the child's guardians counselor, the nanny, the siblings, the social workers versed in ADHD management all play an instrumental role in managing the child's symptoms.

Managing an ADHD child or patient requires a holistic approach, where every part of the child's life is put into perspective and requires maximal attention. These children have a functionally different brain from children of their age; therefore, there is a fundamental difference in behavior mainly due to defect or impaired neurotransmitters that stimulates the prefrontal cortex. The symptoms seen in ADHD children can be seen in a normal child within the same chronological age. Moreover, the difference is that these symptoms persist in children usually more than six months from when the first symptom was noticed. Children with attention deficit hyperactivity disorder confer much stress on their parents and caregiver. Again, since they have a fundamentally different brain and behavior, the parent's or caregiver's behavior should be tweaked to meet the demanding nature of their child's life. This chapter explores how the parent can change their routine behavior to a more intentional and empathetic behavior to meet their child's physical, mental and emotional needs.

To improve your behavior towards your child with ADHD, it's pertinent that you understand completely what ADHD is, such as medications (use of stimulant and nonstimulant), nonpharmacological interventions, behavioral management, and its symptoms as listed by DSM- 5. You can find these symptoms in previous chapters.

Acknowledge the fact that your child or ward has such behavior characteristics and prepare exclusively to help him or her. Psychotherapy would be helpful to better prepare you mentally for the task that is to come. Again, you must understand that it's going to be a stressful and overwhelming task. However, it's going to worth it in the end. Every child deserves the attention of his or her parents regardless of any pathologic situation. Children with ADHD deserve even more and empathetic support.

Short attention span is very common in Attention Deficit Hyperactivity Disorder. They generally have difficulties seating still. As described by experts, their brain lacks a phenomenon in layman terms called filter that is supposed to filter thought and helps one concentrate on one particular thought, multitask, finish through an idea. An ADHD child can imagine more than one hundred different things simultaneously, which implies the child would have little attention on one, jump to the other, and so on. For Instance, Young Andre was diagnosed with ADHD when he was a fifth-grader. His teachers and Guardian counselor were already aware of his diagnosis. While Andre sits in class, he would imagine the color of the sky, how the cloud formed, why his classmates have his hand on his jaw, the size of Gibbs' shoe while trying to grasp what the teacher is illustrating. In the end, he ends up missing out on the information shared in class and also not find out a reasonable answer to all what he was thinking. Research suggests that Andre has a decreased dopamine level and some other neurotransmitters that are supposed to excite the prefrontal cortex that coordinates executive function.

Executive functions are skills that help one plan, focus, judge, and multitask. This facet of ADHD child's brain is greatly impaired. How then can a parent behave in other to manage this dysfunction?

First, the parent needs to be intentional about helping the child in organizing him or herself. Introducing structure into the child's life would do a great deal of help to the child. The structure should be broken into smaller chunks that the child can comprehend and finish quickly. Again, the structure should have a protocol to which the child carries out his discrete activities. For example, the structure should allow adequate time for sleep. Inadequate sleep affects normal people's attention. However, this is even worse for an ADHD child because inadequate sleep aggravates his symptoms. Enough sleep would be helpful in the preceding morning. They may have trouble waking up; the parent should be available to monitor his sleep circle and always interrupt it wherever necessary.

Again, there should be rewards for completing discrete tasks, and there should also be punishment ("cost of choice") for uncompleted tasks. However, be informed that the child would not complete some task, and this is not willful as his misdemeanor is due to a dysfunction that he didn't cause and is still learning how to control. Participating in sport and physical exercise would also help them concentrate more, especially if it's a sport they are passionate about. Sport gives them an avenue to leverage their enormous energy and also improve their motor skills. With these been said, parents should incorporate exercising and planning into their own lives as these would be useful to manage ADHD patients. All these mechanisms would do the child a great deal in heightening his attention span.

Children with ADHD tend to starve as they always miss meals due to hyperactivity and forgetfulness, which is a common symptom of ADHD. While necessary for proper growth and development, food has a central function in building and maintaining healthy tissue in normal children. This is the same as for ADHD children as well. Moreover, inadequate food would deteriorate the growth phases of the child and lead to worse complications. For children on medications, food is important to avert the side effects of some of the drugs. Most drugs for ADHD have side effects that suppress appetites, so adequate meals must be taken to avert the side effects of those drugs, which the parent must modulate. Food is essential for the physical, mental, and psychological development of every young child. It's also crucial that you are flexible with the meal plan. Parents should ensure that meals are taken in the right quantity at the right time. Parents should also prepare meals rich in minerals and vitamins. Again, sugar and caffeine should be excluded in the meals of an ADHD patient as this inhibits their sleep circle, making them inattentive and impulsive when they wake up.

Fidgeting is a common symptom of ADHD. It's characterized by involuntary shaking of body parts. For example, it's an involuntary shaking of the hand or willful stamping of feet. This act can be distracting, especially if the child is in school. Or in a social gathering. This could as well interfere with his or her ability to make friends as his consistent involuntary movement of a body part is usually appalling. Parents or caregivers could assist in this behavior by using a palm weight wrapped around their hands. This makes their hand heavier and thereby reducing fidgety move. There are other fidget tools or toys available commercially that would help in curbing fidgeting.

The behavior of people with ADHD does not go unnoticed. This is true because they don't take turns to speak. They may call out in class or a social setting, which is usually disruptive and annoying for many other students or pupils. Some speak excessively. The teacher and possibly the classmates should be aware of his diagnosis. So when he or she does this, it doesn't come off as much surprise to them. This could also affect the child's social skills. These social skills are important because ADHD patients live in a community of people; therefore, they should be able to obey communal rules like obeying traffic rules, treating others respectfully, and respecting national symbols. The parent can assist here by teaching them how to raise their hand in public when they want to speak. In a bid to improve the child's social skills, the child should be taught how to walk away or report to an adult or teacher whenever he is bothered by his peers. This can be improved in practice by taking the child to a park and monitor how he or she behaves in such a community of people. He should also be rewarded when he acts fair and respectfully.

In conclusion, raising an ADHD child can be daunting. However, it's imperative that you put your mental health in perspective because a mentally challenged person cannot manage an ADHD child. As an ADHD parent, you're not alone. Take rest where necessary, go on a walk, seek professional advice from your community and a professional social worker with expertise in ADHD management. Acknowledge that your child's behavior is not willful. Treat him or her with empathy, this would foster trust, and he or she would heed your instructions when they can trust you.

2.6 Managing Relationship Between an ADHD Child and Siblings or Pets

This book has mainly focused on parents of children with ADHD and the need to be well-informed to help manage their illnesses. In this chapter, our focus will be on siblings of children with ADHD, because they also play a key role in managing this condition.

As a parent of a child with ADHD, you cannot avoid learning ways to effectively deal with your child's behavior. It is important to ensure that while you are learning strategies to cope and manage the condition, you do not leave siblings in the dark. If a child with ADHD has other siblings, those siblings are also likely to face difficulties in many ways. For example, they may not be able to fully understand why their families face certain difficulties compared to other families. One of the major problems with most families is sibling rivalry, and this can become extremely challenging, especially when one such child has ADHD.

Ryan Willimas is a child diagnosed with ADHD. Each time a family friend pays them a visit, 11-year-old Ryan is usually the only one, out of his 4 siblings to ask if the visitor will like a cup of water or biscuit. This is a classical behavior of children with ADHD. They usually tend to be articulate, loving, bright, and imaginative.

However, Ryan also has a higher tendency to crash his bike into his older brother, burst into a room uninvited, or snatch a toy from his younger sister. One minute, Ryan is a gentleman, and the next minute, he's provoking everyone, says his mom.

Also, his mom reports that he also has a problem maintaining focus, and is unable to stay still, especially when he is bored.

- **Rivalry at Home:** It is completely a normal thing for families to experience sibling rivalry. However, when one such child has ADHD, disagreements tend to be more wearisome and frequent. The main issue is that these kids with ADHD are usually quick to misjudge social situations. They are usually impatient and tend to interrupt conversations without invitations. Children with ADHD also speak loudly, and they do other inappropriate and silly things that can embarrass their parents and siblings. That is why most families resort to excluding their kids with ADHD. The bad news for their siblings is that they may be sidelined as well. Siblings may also feel some resentment toward the ADHD child because they usually receive more attention from their parents.

- **Support for Siblings:** Providing support for siblings of children with ADHD can be difficult because of the behavior that these children exhibit is often regarded as attention-seeking or bad behaviors. The siblings of a child with ADHD are usually subject to negative media messages, and this can have a negative impact on how they understand what the ADHD child is going through. Therefore, it is important to ensure that the siblings are able to recognize the fact that the ADHD child has a disorder, rather than allowing them to live with the idea that they are just being stubborn.

2.6.1   ADHD Sibling

It is your duty as a parent of a child with ADHD to also ensure that their siblings are able to cope with the condition. Here are some ways that you can help non-ADHD kids cope with their siblings as well as the family dynamic:

1. It may be tough to make the time, but try to fit in extra non-ADHD time: This may be a difficult feat to do, but you must give your full attention to the non-ADHD kid the same as you give to the ADHD child. Most parents often face an issue that they concentrate more on the child with ADHD, overlooking other children.. This is an unhealthy thing to do, and it can only cause the non-ADHD child to feel sidelined, or think their siblings are attention-seeking. While you are following up with your ADHD child and ensuring that they get better, you equally need to ensure that the non-ADHD child gets all the positive nurturing and attention they need.

2. Don't hide the condition from non-ADHD children: Ensure that all your children know the condition, as well as the challenges they are likely to face with their ADHD sibling. These challenges are usually more when it comes to time management, and controlling other ADHD symptoms.

3. Work with your non-ADHD child: Without working with your non-ADHD children, they won't know how to deal with problematic behaviors from the child with ADHD. You need to work with the non-ADHD child to teach them how to handle such behaviors. There are several strategies that you can employ to achieve this.

You can sit the non-ADHD child and brainstorm together, you can even use role-play strategies to achieve this. The aim is to ensure that the non-ADHD child is able to automatically and naturally respond in a loving manner to whatever behavior the child with ADHD exhibits.

4. Be understanding and emphatic with the non-ADHD child, especially when they are having trouble handling their ADHD siblings. It is usually difficult for these kids to act in order when the siblings with ADHD exhibit provoking behaviors. Don't be quick to rebuke them if this happens because it will only make them more rebellious.

5. Ensure that you structure your home such that it is ADHD-friendly. You can set specific routines, use clear rules and consequences, lots of praise, frequent feedback, and more. With this, you can help the child stay proactive and help their siblings manage the difficult symptoms of ADHD.

2.7 Learn to be empath with your kid

Childrearing is often tedious and requires a lot of trial and error, especially if you're a first-time parent. These trials and errors may affect the child's perception of his community, people, and resources around him. In psychology, the nature vs. nurture argument equally applies to children. The nature argument holds that a child's behavior is controlled from within- that is, the genetic constituents transferred from parent to offspring. On the other hand, the Nurture argument holds that the environment plays a significant role in the child's behavior. The nurture school of thought put into consideration the context of social, cultural, and socioeconomic status. The social context of the nurture argument says that a child's interaction with his peers and family members could influence the child's life positively or negatively, as the case may be. The cultural context emphasizes that the culture a child is born into influences his morals, values, sense of obligation, respect for rules and law, to mention a few. Finally, the socioeconomic context reviews how the amount of money a child's parent earns, their neighborhood, and the quality of meals a child gets influences his behaviors.

People with higher socioeconomic levels have greater access to opportunities than people at the lower part of the scale. Researchers have concluded that nature and nurture debate plays a 50/50 role in the child's development around the context of behavior. The popular way of parenting has always been a consequence of how one was patented. Children across culture, location, and socioeconomic level behave distinctly. Therefore, there are no universal tips for rearing a child to achieve insights, empathy, and repair. The goal of parenting falls greatly on raising children: ' citizens and citizens leaders' Who treat others with respect and honor regardless of age and socioeconomic status. And sees all humans as deserving of dignity. This part explores tips to achieve this.

First, it's important to establish what your goals and purpose of childbirth and rearing are. It involves asking questions like;

- What kind of parent do I want to be?
- What type of relationship do I want to establish between myself and my children?
- What level of trust do I want between myself and my ward?
- What legacies do I want to leave for my children?
- What image of the world do I want to create for my children?

It involves answering the above-mentioned questions and more. Childrearing is a daunting task as it involves the parents' financial, mental, psychological, cultural, physical, and spiritual preparedness. Which, when not in place, can derail you from the set goals. However, these set goals should be accompanied by specific, actionable plans to achieve these goals while maintaining the flexibility and autonomy of the child. Your goals should be effective enough to put the child's rights, health, and aspirations into perspective. The goal should give the children an avenue to explore the world in its entirety and make an informed decision based on the lesson they have learned from you. Your system of achieving set goals involves mental exercise, primacy, futuristic plans, pervasive, and open-mindedness. As Myles Munroe puts it, "When the purpose is not known, abuse is enviable." When you have a purpose, you will stay on course even when the child's behavior is not aligning. Days like this will arise; it's your purpose and goal that would sustain you.

Secondly, redefine discipline- "induction" over "power assertion." There have been several schools of thought as regard parenting. The most popular being the "spare the rod and spoil the child" school of thought and the "free to be you and me" school of thought. Even though both systems have its flaw and merits, it doesn't apply to all children across culture, geographic location, and socioeconomic status. Discipline in the 21st century had lost its original meaning. When a mom says to her child, I will discipline you! What comes to your mind? Let me guess; I'm guessing you would think spank, flog with a cane (as in an African setting), deprive the child of Some certain rights and privileges like 'turn off the movie now and go to bed- early bedtime. Discipline is being seen as a way to correct the child's actions, and in our modern world, we tend to correct out of impulse, which is flawed. Take, for instance, your child acts out of impulse and causes a tantrum which infuriates you; then, you, the parent acts out of infuriation (impulse) by ceasing his or her toys or sending him or her to bed early, cutting short his screen time, which annoys the child. Both parties go away angry.

Here, you can obviously see that the system of punishment is flawed. Empathy and human interconnectedness have not been established. Virtually all families crave connectedness and empathy; this is truly possible only when we slow down a bit and put ourselves in the shoes of the other person, whether a child or an adult. Discipline from Latin means disciplina, which means to teach, instruct, and direct. This word originated far back in the eleventh century. Suppose the old and still valuable definition of discipline is applied in the above scenario. You would see that the purpose of discipline has been missed. Therefore, it's pertinent that the parents redefine what discipline is. The goal of discipline is to make the child independent in action and behavior and be able to choose between good and bad behaviors, whether In the presence or absence of their parents.

The ultimate goal of the parent is to raise children that can thrive outside the confinement of their home, where there are high expectations on their character and personality. To impact a child positively amidst tantrums, what should a parent do? According to the "No-drama Discipline" book, the following three questions are essential in finding discipline: What happened to my child? In this time, what lesson do I want to convey? To effectively instruct the group, how should I approach this lesson? For instance, Justin's Mom returned home from a long day at work. She works in a publishing company where she performed a bunch of typing and editing. Before she dropped Justin at school, she promised him a cup of ice cream and some bar of chocolate. Justin, out of excitement, hugs his Mom, says his final goodbye and runs into his school to meet his class teacher and peers. Justin's Mom watched her son run into the school with a generous smile. When her son was out of sight, she shook her head and murmured in amazement how childhood could be very funny. She shot the car door that Justin left through and drove off. It's a nice and tedious day at work; she told her husband as she walked into the room. Suddenly, it was Justin running towards the Mom with excitement and expectation as well, after they exchanged pleasantries and enquiring about school. Justin finally broke the ice by asking, Mummy, where is my ice cream? The Mom, with her palm on her face, said, oh! My God! Not again.

I forgot to buy it, Justin. The woman was already worried, Justin out of infatuation, was already working out on his Mom in annoyance. The Mom finally called him back; it's a prank, she whined. Mummy! Really? He said, working back to receive his ice cream reluctantly, already smiling. When he opened it, he yelled Mom, you got the wrong flavor, and he immediately dropped the cup of ice cream on the floor, making a mess of the sitting room. The Mom got so pissed like every other parent and cleaned up the mess, took the child in, and changed his clothes.

I guess Justin's Mom must have acted contrary to what you expected. However, her reaction was based on her ability to ask the above-mentioned questions before reacting. She acted out of "curiosity and not assumptions." Curiosity explores the question of why did my child do this- For Justin, it must have been out of disappointment. He acted out of impulsiveness, and the parent, remembering the goal she had set regarding his behaviors, acted that way at the cool of the event. Justin's Mom told the son, I understand how you feel at the moment, and it must have been tough for you; please note that it's wrong for you to waste food. Even if you don't like it, don't squander food. Justin felt loved, and he learned not to waste food even though he didn't like it

The Mom's response to his son is called induction. According to Psychology by Carole Wade and Carol Tavris, induction is defined as a method of child parenting where the parent use techniques that appeal to children's capabilities, values, and compassion towards others in reining in disobedience. Here the Mom appeals to Justin about how she felt as regard his action, which was a medium of teaching Justin to put other person's feeling first before reacting as opposed to power assertion, which is scolding or spanking the child as a means of disciplining him because there are stronger and bigger than the child. With Justin's Mom's reaction, you see empathy and connectedness have been built, and discipline served.

Thank you for purchasing my book. I have 2 GIFTS FOR YOU: MY audiobook and a free video course regarding "How To Discipline Your Child with ADHD". You can download these materials for free from this link: https://dl.bookfunnel.com/b8yw5x4m7t

2.8 Parenting errors

Parenting is daunting. There is no doubt! Deciding the appropriate disciplinary options specific for your children without being mean and disconnected from your children is even more tasking. Discipline is from the root word disciples; it refers to teaching and instructing your followers using appropriate consequences for their actions. Discipline is proof of love. There is no perfect parenting guide available. In disciplining your child, you want him to be cooperative with you as the parent and also prepare him to face the praises and consequences of their actions in the future. However, some disciplinary mechanism may not be in your child's best interest, in the long run, therefore, should be avoided. Your child is different. Therefore, they will require a different discipline approach from that of the previous children you've had, and this should be with consistent praise and consequences for one's action. This should be done fairly, Friendly, and firmly considering the child's age and developmental stage. Parenting requires flexibility.

Thinking short-term disciplining. Discipline that seeks immediate cooperation alone should be avoided. Discipline is aimed at teaching and providing the child with appropriate knowledge and skills to enable him or her to make an informed decision now and in the future. Seeking cooperation instantaneously means you're teaching the child how to be sneakier. How to hide their behavior in order not to get caught. For instance, you have warned your child against playing soccer after school so he has enough time to do his assignments and household chores before bedtime. Previously, he played football from 3 pm when he returned from school till 6 pm; as a consequence of his over-involvement in the sport, he got fatigued and missed dinner, his assignments, and the Family's favorite television show that served as a bonding time for the Family for that day. You warned him against such an act, to which he Intermittently agreed. Next time, he played the sport, stopping at the time you were supposed to be back from work. So he pretends like nothing happened that day; you thought he complied and never mentioned it. He doses off during his favorite TV show and doesn't contribute to the usual dining discourse. Well! With the best intentions, you thought his drowsiness was a result of the tedious day he had in school. So you were less worried. One eventful day at work, you received an emergency call to rush to a local clinic within your neighborhood that your son was involved in an accident that led to the fracture of his left arm as a result of the soccer you warned him against. Now, the parents are angry and can't lash out because he is already in severe pain. The scenario is not unpopular. As a parent, this wouldn't feel well with you. Think about discipline in the short term and the long-term reaction to prevent such repercussions. Make it as explicit as possible. Show him why he must not spend too much time on soccer and leave out other essential things. Let him or she understand that soccer is not bad, but too much of it can affect other important activities like family time, academics, and even his or her future relationships.

Inconsistency in discipline would be detrimental to the child's behavior and would halt essential connection with the parent. Therefore, it should be avoided or discontinued if already in practice. Discipline is essential to childrearing. It has already been established that discipline is a process of teaching and instructing a child. However, when the child's behavior is not in line with the teaching, it should be tantamount to punishment. Punishment is a mechanism of letting the child understand that there is a penalty for every action executed by anyone, and it could be either good or bad. Again, this punishment should be what it is. The importance of consistent punishment is that it would make the child understand that outside the house, the community or society demand high expectations on his personality, and wherever, he defaults he would be duly punished for his ineptitude. Again, this would also make him or her take your words for it and not just bluffs.

For instance, a mom driving home from a nature park she took her children to. On their way home, she looked through the rear mirror of her car and noticed her eldest son, that's eight years old, playing with a heavy toy in the back seat. It didn't seem to be a problem until the eldest son started hovering the toy over the head of his two sleeping sisters. The mom warned! 'Stop that! If it lands on your sisters, it will hurt them,' and if this happens, you won't see that toy for one month. If this eventually happens and the mom does nothing, the child may not take his mom seriously again. You don't want your child not taking you seriously.

Therefore, punishments should be followed through consistently and lovingly. Some factors may become a hindering block to you following through on your punishment regimens, such as pitying your child, not wanting to see your child cry or the feeling of guilt on the parent's side. However, it's better to correct a bad behavior than letting them grow with an obnoxious behavior that might put him on the wrong side of the Constitution or law of the country he resides in. Inconsistency could arise when both parents don't agree on the same discipline approach. Having a discipline plan is valuable. However, when either the parent or both of the parents don't stick to the plan, it aggravates the teaching/discipline techniques. The parent should have a plan that works for both of them. Plans are important for monitoring or evaluating growth and development.

The lies that parents tell in order to discipline and motivate their children isn't worth it and should be avoided greatly. It's not uncommon to hear a parent yelling at their child, saying, 'when I was your age, I used to do this, I use to do that, and on and on.' This does more harm than good. It puts unnecessary pressure on your child. It also gives your child a negative view of failure instead of seeing it as feedback that requires attention. Failure is part of our existence; we miss some point, then we bounce back better if we strategize and take action. So when you lie about your position in class in time past, you're simply destroying the kid's self-esteem. These discipline mistakes should be avoided. For instance, Jessica performed poorly in school. When she got home, she already felt remorseful about her results; then, her parents were not home at that time. When her parents finally arrived home that day from work. Jessica presented her scorecard to her parents. The parent got pissed and yelled at her, saying things like, when I was your age, I came best in my class. The people in your class are human like you. Just imagine if Jessica later finds out that her dad lied about her results or performance in high school. There is a high propensity that she would not believe her dad again. Honesty is always the best policy. Again, comparing your child or ward to other children is very toxic and should not be attempted. This cliché "Comparison is the thief of joy" is valid in this case. The long-term effect of comparing your child to another wouldn't be fair. Your child is unique, with a unique prowess or potential that needs to be harnessed and plugged into the right source for adequate pruning and growth.

Pseudo-discipline. Some parents want to prove to their friends or relatives that they can put wrong behavior in control in seconds. Nonetheless, you may end up proving your point, but in the long run, you're hurting your child and not genuinely caring for them as you intended. The child's actions you would normally ignore because people you respect are around you then tend to act out of impulse, forgetting your plans. This form of discipline should be avoided. It destroys your child's esteems and may hurt his or her relationship with other people in the future. Another aftermath of this type of discipline is that it doesn't give your children the opportunity to network with your friend's Family, which may halt profitable potential connections between both families. The goal, however, is to ensure that bad behavior doesn't persist, and this should be done intentionally and communicated properly to enable the child to believe that his best interest is central to your discipline plan. Discipline should be done empathetically. However, pseudo-discipline doesn't allow that. These discipline types include but not limited to the following; yelling, spanking, timeout, shaming, on and on. This type of behavior causes the child to be ashamed of who he or she is and could make her underachieve in the long run, which no thoughtful parent wants.

"The Whole-Brain Child" book Contains methods for improving human connection, empathy, and relationship formation through better understanding how your child's brain functions. Experiences define the kind of brain the child grows with, and the parent is a great determinant. In the book, the child's brain is divided into four parts, namely, the Left-brain that coordinates logic, reasoning, handwriting, analysis, Science, and math. The right brain expresses emotions, creativity, imagination, intuition, insights, and nonverbal cues. The downstairs brain acts before thinking, and the upstairs brain coordinates executive functions.

The goal is to make your child function effectively with all the parts of their brains. This can be done by a process called integration. Integration helps for full self-awareness, control emotions, improved decision making, a great relationship, and good academic performance. Stay focused on this book's principle by connecting with your children emotionally, as logic won't work when your child or the parent and the child are both angry. Allow them to tell how they feel about different situations and tame it when necessary. Engage with your children; children love to be listened to. Listening to them would help you solve the problem empathetically rather than being reactive. Focus on making them understand how they feel things around them, images, and thoughts. Focus on making them understand that their feelings are temporal and valid. Body movements would help them create balance in their brain and relaxes them as well. The brain parts are like a muscle; it gets better when we stretch it, so do our behaviors. Engaging them mentally would do a lot of benefits for them. Help them remember things that happened in the past; this would improve their brain ability.

In conclusion, there is no specific manual for parenting; the parents are laden with the bulk of specific discoveries for their child. However, the discipline techniques should help you connect emotionally with your child, then take them away from the malpractice. A term that the authors of the Whole Brain Child calls "Connect and redirect." When you're able to do this, you're telling the child that you're against his bad behavior and not the child. This technique fosters empathy which is key in relating with other people in society. It's overwhelming to follow through on rewards or punishment for our child's misdemeanor. However, this is essential in establishing the fact that there are consequences for one's action at home and outside the fence of the house. The feeling of pity, guilt and unfairness may set in when trying to exact adequate consequences on the child, therefore, the relevance of a flexible plan. A discipline plan shows growth and improvement.

Nonetheless, "honesty is the best policy" tell the truth to your child at all times. Always consider your child's age and developmental stages when exacting consequences for their actions; remember that some part of their brain has not been fully developed and requires integration to function maximally at some certain age. Be kind, affectionate, and flexible with your discipline approach.

Thank you for purchasing my book. I have 2 GIFTS FOR YOU: MY audiobook and a free video course regarding "How To Discipline Your Child with ADHD". You can download these materials for free from this link: https://dl.bookfunnel.com/b8yw5x4m7t

3   MANAGING YOUR CHILD'S CONDITION

3.1   How You Are Reinforcing Negative Behavior Without Even Knowing It

As parents, we show our love and care in the best way we can and know how to do best. It is our joy to see our children succeed and be the best in whatever they find themselves doing. It is our duty to correct, love, and protect our kids. We never want to see our children go in the wrong direction. However, we need to be sure that we are showing love to our kids the right way.

Can our actions affect and reinforce negative behavior without us realizing it and even with our purest intention? The truth is that we are humans, and sometimes our good intention may actually be exposing our kids to behavior and characters that are unhealthy. Children are known to be great imitators of actions they see, hear or perceive and the same way they learn to say the words they hear from us, eat the things they see us eating, and are intently watching unconsciously to learn is the same way they can learn negative behavior from us without us realizing.

A child brought up in a home where both parents fight and lack respect for each other will most likely grow up disrespecting his or her spouse until he decides to unlearn the behavior. The parents didn't sit him down to say, this is how to disrespect your wife per se, but they were able to influence his behavior even without them realizing it. Another way we as parents reinforce negative behavior without knowing is by refusing to correct our children when they are wrong; when I say correct, I mean correction with love whenever we see them go on wrong paths and let them have their way, we are reinforcing negative behavior without realizing. For instance, I see my son take things that don't belong to him, and I let him have his way because I really don't want to make him feel bad or be rash, I am unconsciously encouraging the behavior, and it may progress, and correction may be hard later on.

In cases where we raise our voices to correct our children or wards, we might be exposing them to fear of expressing themselves in difficult situations. We compare our kids to folks their age to make them see that they can better and not complacent in their fields; we introduce envy and imposter syndrome because they will most likely feel that they are not good enough and nothing they ever do will.

Most times, hurtful body-shaming comments and remarks are most likely from parents because they want you to watch what you eat and take in, but these comments end up making them feel less amazing than they are, and yet most of these comments and remarks may seem harmless, it takes a long time to get over and heal from.

Yes, we are good parents. Yes, we want the best for our wards, but we may be doing more harm than good without even realizing it.

The big question can parenting affect ADHD

As parents, we might reinforce negative behavior without realizing it, but good or bad parenting really doesn't cause this disorder but has a huge effect on managing this disorder.

The ways you can reinforce negative behavior in children with ADHD include

· **Saying negative things to the child**

Your child has a disorder doesn't mean you shouldn't love and care like you will do for a child without ADHD. Treat all children with respect disorder or not.

· **Focusing on their weakness rather than on their strength**

Your child may lose focus most of the time and find it very difficult to concentrate, and instead of focusing on the thing they are doing wrong, give them credit sometimes, make them feel special, encourage and spot out their strength and help them get better in their weaknesses.

· **Comparing their progress**

Children with ADHD find it very hard to focus, unlike other children, so it is not wise to use this against them. Instead of comparing them to other kids, be patient with them and be intentional about their growth. It may be slow, but trust me when I say that there will be improvements if you put in the work.

· **Having unreasonable expectations**

A child finding it difficult to pay attention to details needs constant reminders on what you want them to achieve.

Expecting them to know what to do every time is like unreasonable and unachievable expectations. Even children without ADHD are prone to forgetting instructions and needs constant reminder that you need to do this or that. For children with ADHD, it takes extra effort to make them understand what is expected of them.

· **Not spending time with your children**

Coming to terms that your child has a disorder may be quite overwhelming and might make you start ignoring their wants and needs. The truth is that your child needs you now more than ever, make them feel wanted and expected from home because they might have a tough time connecting with the world outside, but when they experience love and care from home, it makes their journey seamless and easy.

Would you please encourage them to engage in stimulating activities and allow yourself to offer them your full attention? Then, finally, approach and praise them when they have a minor victory.

Not understanding the way ADHD affects your child

When you don't have adequate knowledge of this disorder, many things could go wrong because you don't understand the situation. Study everything you can about ADHD; follow all treatment sessions suggested to you. Always give your kid their medication on schedule. When your doctor is out of town, always double-check the dosage. To ensure your child's medications stay where they should, put them in a secure location where others cannot get them.

I understand that it can be a bit overwhelming as a parent who wants the best for their child, you can get stressed and frustrated many times and lash out, but in this journey, you are not in this alone; you can take time out to catch your breath rest.

You can also join support groups and communities of parents in the same situation as you. You would be surprised at the number of things you could learn.

3.2 Managing ADHD at Home and at School

"It takes a village to raise a child," they say. The task of Child rearing comes with its challenges and merits. Parenting children with ADHD is even more stressful and challenging. However, it can be walked through with the right information and empathy. Empathy is really important in bringing up a normal child, and it's even more important when dealing with a child diagnosed with ADHD. Because they act out of impulse and you reacting with impulse as well doesn't help matters; rather, it aggravates it. Therefore, empathy will go a long way in dealing with the child and help the parent reduce stress since they feel and understand what the child is going through. The right information is also needed to avert or combat the negative effects of bad behavior. The most accurate information can be gotten from the child's village. The village required to raise an ADHD child is the child's pediatricians, a clinical psychologist with expertise in ADHD, the school management, the class teacher, the parents, caregivers (Babysitter or nanny), family, and friends. This set of people help make the environment where the child resides or interacts with ADHD friendly. For there to be full cooperation amongst these sets of people, they need to be well informed about the child's diagnosis. Also, they should be aware of the child's strengths and weaknesses. Managing a child with ADHD requires intentionality from all the groups involved. Again, since the child will be mainly at school and home, the bulk of the work falls on the parent, the school management, and the class teacher. Therefore, this chapter explores how to manage ADHD at home and in school.

Firstly, the structure is key in the house where the child with ADHD resides. Actionable plans and structures are essential in helping the child develop skills that will help him thrive at school, work, and relationships with others. People with ADHD often have an impaired prefrontal cortex that coordinates executive function. The executive function is crucial for planning, focusing, finishing a task, controlling emotions, mental flexibility, etc. When these essential skills are functionally impaired, the parents and caregivers automatically become a helping hand to help the child plan, coordinate and finish the task. The first step in tackling a challenge is by identifying the challenges. The parent should identify specific problems their child is going through. When identified, they can then proceed to develop a flexible and empathetic structure that supports the child's development. Researchers use the phrase "functionally different brain" to describe the type of brain that children or adults with ADHD have. This means that they are often bombarded with multiple thoughts at the same time, therefore, unable to follow through on tasks and quizzes as in a school setting. This means the parent should follow their child care one step at a time. Overloading them with responsibilities would be overwhelming to them and equally make them unable to focus. Therefore, parents should break tasks into tiny chunks that the child can understand and implement. In as much as you want your child to readily follow through on all your instructions, make room for mistakes. For instance, if your child is supposed to be doing his home chores, then you found him playing with his toys or causing a tantrum. Don't react out of frustration, rather with warmth, carefully remind him what he should be doing at that particular time and redirect him to what is needful. There would be a time when he would behave in a way that doesn't align with your expectations, be reminded that his behaviors are not willful. Again, in dealing with a child with ADHD, it's best to make expectations, rewards, and discipline approaches consistent. This would help him realize that there is an aftermath for one's action, whether good or bad. Being inconsistent with expectations, rewards, and a disciplined approach would only make him or her take your words for granted. The consistency in expectations, rewards, and discipline approach should be consistent across the board. This implies that the parents, teacher, grandparent, and the babysitter should follow the same disciplined approach consistently.

Children with ADHD exude so much energy. Sporting activities give them the avenue to express themselves. Again, children with ADHD may be socially incompetent that's they lack basic social skills that are required to build and sustain relationships, they're usually unable to start a new relationship, read body language, and so on. This impact adversely on their ability to mingle with other kids. So, sporting activities like Martial arts that are structured and have many rules applied could teach the child self-control and patience. Again, group sports like volleyball, American football, basketball, and so on teaches the child to work in a group while enjoying the sport. Those group sports help them concentrate their energies, develop self and social awareness essential in building friends. Exercises give them an avenue to hone how to delay gratification for future benefits. That's taming their impulsive urge for the benefit of the team. Again, exercise improves sleep.

Furthermore, children with ADHD have issues coordinating how much time they spend on activities. It's either they spend more time than necessary on activities, especially if they are passionate about such activity, or less time doing different unnecessary activities. Hence, the need for a planner. The parent can make a list of rules that apply to their child's special needs and then paste it on the wall of his room. It helps the child stay focused by reminding him what he is expected to do at a particular time. He or she would default to some of the rules, therefore be flexible and correct with warmth and love. Corrections aim to show the child how to do it better than he previously did. So yelling, spanking, hitting, and timeout may not be the best approach for a child with neurodevelopmental dysfunction like ADHD. Planners help break the activities down into smaller chunks that are understandable. Again, children with ADHD cannot control how much time they spend on television and other activities. Sometimes they stay so long on television that they forget their chores, assignments, and important activities there were supposed to be on.

Nonetheless, as a parent, having to deal with an ADHD child can be stressful and overwhelming. You must seek help from your colleagues or family when expressing burnouts. It takes a mentally stable and socially aware person to bring up a child with ADHD. When overwhelmed, you can take a walk in the park, go hiking, and biking. Employ a nanny to help you whenever you feel inundated due to stress. Therapy is a good way to relieve yourself of stress and be informed professionally on alleviating suffering on your child.

Managing ADHD in school

The parent at school cannot monitor the child's conduct. The kid has connections with other school members and class members who cannot react as kindly as feasible. Therefore, the baton falls on the hand of the school management and the child's classroom teacher to take care of the child with special needs and other students. This can be overwhelming as the teacher may have more than one child with special needs to look out for. The school psychologist and counselor could be of great help. Combined with teaching and other staff activities. However, there are efficient ways to manage children with

ADHD. Individuals with ADHD often miss out in class as a result of their inability to focus or pay attention, Hyperactivity, and Impulsivity. Sometimes very disruptive, not because they intend to. However, these symptoms can be managed.

First, the teacher and school management need to establish a working relationship with the parent. It's only through the parent that the child's diagnosis can be confirmed. Again, the teacher needs adequate information about the child's strengths and weaknesses beyond what is already known in school. This relationship is important in following through rewards, expectations, and corrections consistently. Again, this relationship is essential as it facilitates an easy flow of information between the school and the child's parents. It's not a bad idea that the child's classmates know about the child's diagnosis. The essence of this is to create a more compassionate buddy and ADHD-friendly environment for the child. Shared positivity is vital for both the child and his college to thrive. If his or her fellow pupils are aware of his medical condition, they would be able to tolerate one another and not take his or her shortcomings as a willful act.

The teacher should bring the child with ADHD closer to his or her desk; this helps reduce visual distractions from his colleagues and facilitate easy communication. This would limit the rate of engagement from other students that may be distracting. The teacher should communicate clearly and frequently to help the child coordinate things himself. The use of visual representation to communicate to the child is proven to be helpful. The visual representation may indicate when to start an activity or end one. As a result of Impulsivity, the child may have a hard time sitting still; therefore, they should be allowed to take a walk at intervals and do some exercise as well. This provides an avenue for the child to exact their energy. Putting students close to the door, window, and close to a talkative buddy is quite detrimental to their improvement. It's best to put them away from possible distractions. In most cases, fidgety tools are important as it helps them stay calm, especially when hyperactive. It's accurate to ensure that those fidgety tools are not becoming a source of distraction to the child, mostly when there is an ongoing lesson.

It is challenging for children with ADHD to begin and complete their tasks, mainly when they are significant and repeatable. Therefore, the instructor may organize tasks in a manner that is child-specific. A breakdown of steps on how the assignments should be done would help the child organize and focus on the work at hand. Again, children with special needs should be given extra time on assignments and quizzes, which allows them more time to start, pause and continue the assignment or quiz until it's completed. Most of the time, they may get poor grades which might wreck their confidence. The best approach to help them regain confidence is by asking them questions within their strength; this helps rejuvenate their confidence in class. Positive reinforcement would improve the child's behavior, and the practice of rewarding good behavior would encourage the child greatly.

In conclusion, effective communication between the parent, teacher, school teacher, school psychologist, and the members of the family is important for the management of an ADHD child. The task of helping to manage the child's condition falls heavily on the above-mentioned individuals. It's not the intention of an ADHD child to cause trouble in their neighborhood. However, the defect in the prefrontal cortex and reduced level of dopamine affects their ability to focus, plan and complete the task. The members of the class are vital as well in helping the child thrive in school. Therefore, the class teacher should orientate them about ADHD positively to avoid any chances of bullying from other students. Structure is very important in managing ADHD, and the parent has to be proactive, empathetic, and caring. ADHD management requires feedback. The child's behavior amongst peers should be watched, and this would show if there has been a significant behavioral change; this is important as the child doesn't know how his behaviors affect others. The most effective method to organize a playdate is to host it with your neighbor's or coworker's children. Use this to identify changes in social skills and any improvements to those abilities. It is critical to have good social skills to form and sustain a connection. This ability is crucial because it helps the kid resist social isolation, which has a pronounced impact.

3.3 Social Skills Therapy Techniques

ADHD symptoms have a devastating effect on social skills. People with ADHD often have a hard time relating with peers and maintaining such relationships as they're often inattentive, impulsive, and hyperactive. Many people with ADHD don't take turns in conversation or shared activities as a result of Impulsivity and hyperactivity. Social skills are behavior that is essential in understanding and observing verbal and nonverbal cues used in relating and communicating effectively with other people. Humans are generally gregarious beings; being unable to socialize with one's peers and community harms the mental health and the esteem of the person as loneliness could lead to the person wanting to join any group that accepts him, whether good or detrimental. Social isolation is tantamount to death as one could become suicidal or addicted to hard substances. Establishing eye contact, knowing when the person is not being receptive to the current discourse and wants a change, expressing your opinions aptly and in turn listening to the other parties speak, acknowledging how others feel and putting yourself in their shoes, sharing in other people's emotions appropriately, for instances, laughing with them when they're laughing and crying with them when they're in dismay, and initiating and upholding a conversation. The above-listed are examples of essential social skills and more required to relate with peers positively. People that use the above-mentioned Social skills to relate and enhance relationships are said to be socially competent. The impairment of the prefrontal cortex that modulates executive functions wreaks havoc on the child's attempt to socialize with his peers. ADHD poses a threat to one's ability to be likable, socialize, and maintain the relationship. They often act out impulsive and hyperactive, which are inappropriate in a community of people. Most people don't realize that this is a skill, therefore, can be learned. Although, it requires time, patience, and intentionality. This chapter seeks to expatiate how to improve social skills therapy in ADHD children.

Firstly, teach your child how to respond when a conflict arises between him and his peers. An example of such a response could be reporting to a teacher or higher authorities, especially when not within the school vicinity. Social skills vary from people, cultures, and location, endeavors to consciously help him learn the social rules applicable in his Community. Help him practice interacting with people of different backgrounds. This helps him see the world beyond his immediate environment. Again, teachers can be very helpful in helping an ADHD child develop some essentially impaired social skills. ADHD patients usually have issues with classes. Should the child fail or miss out on quizzes. The teacher can help him increase his self-esteem by allowing him to answer questions on the board in front of his colleagues that he or she is sure that is within the strength of the child. This helps reduces the feeling of fear and puts him in the best position to mingle with his classmates.

Nonetheless, pairing Children with other humane children can also help improve their social skills. These children are usually often trained by a social worker that has expertise in ADHD management. This social worker inculcates adequate skills that the other child would need to relate well with the ADHD child in his team. The ADHD child benefits greatly because he doesn't feel socially awkward any longer, which greatly improves his confidence in interacting with other peers. The scenario above is similar to that of Russell's case. Russell, a California-Born, has already been diagnosed with ADHD at an early age and is already undergoing psychotherapy since the medication wasn't working for him. He would often isolate himself since any attempt to befriend someone always proves abortive. Therefore, he ventured into substance abuse in other to keep his emotions up. His community already labeled him as a social misfit. He didn't get along with friends compared to people within his age bracket. Russell's mom was observant enough to report her child's misdemeanor to a social worker. After his diagnosis, he was recommended to start a session with a support group. On arrival at the venue of the support group's meeting. He was immediately paired with a trained, compassionate buddy. James became more interested in Russell's growth and development. They would do some sport together such as running, weight lifting, and hiking. Soon Russell started to come out of his shell gradually. He often told James how he felt about some activities around him, what he believes would have made sense. This particularly elevated their bonding. James, a trained personnel, never felt tired of Russell's inconsistent behaviors; rather, with empathy and genuine concern, James followed through with Russell. They became intimate friends even outside the walls of their support group venue. In one of their evaluation and feedback meetings. Russell's mom was full of Joy as a result of Russell's growth and improvement. Through the meeting, he discovered the sport that sparked his creativity, Russell's mom said. Pairing your child to a buddy helps develop compassionate citizens who know the relevance of human interconnectedness and lifelong friends who are open to helping the child walk through their social phobias. It could serve as a means to develop one's inner creativity, just as Russell did. Again, as a parent, you're your child's mentor and role model. The parent should ensure that he or she is portraying the essential social skills he is demanding from the child. This would foster trust and resilience.

Often, children with ADHD don't clearly understand how their behavior impacts others around them; therefore, it's pertinent that you as a parent should be able to serve as a coach that watches them play, then recommend and implement adequate growth strategies for your son or daughter. You must deliver accurate, detailed, and clear feedback that the child can work with. Again, their reaction or behavior is not intentional; their behavior results from functional dysfunction in the brain, which they may not have caused. As a parent or caregiver, it's pertinent that you teach them to be socially and self-aware. They should understand that people feel happy or sad based on their reaction to several social cues. Being socially aware is being able to understand how you fit into a community, alongside how others fit into such community, and being able to use how they want to be represented to relate with them. Social awareness is essential in building and maintaining positive friendships. This is a skill one develops from childhood through adulthood. It's pretty simple for an open-minded individual to alter their way of life without drastically impacting the well-being of their neighborhood. To improve their social skills, the ADHD child needs to be provided with feedback on any miscue they have done. The best way to monitor and correct this is miscue is by taking them on a play date where they are allowed to interact with other kids. The playdates should be in a small group, as large group may be distracting and overwhelming for him or her. Nonetheless, their behaviors toward other kids and the way other kids interpreted or responded to his body language should be noted and corrected if need be. These corrections and expectations should be clear and consistent.

Roleplaying is a vital way of improving social skills; especially, in a classroom setting. Roleplay can be deployed at home as well. Roleplaying is a method of learning that has to do with different members of a class delivering a particular task assigned to them by the instructor or teacher. This activity is coordinated so that the participants would contribute or play their roles at a specified time. Then the other members of the group would react to the person's perspective. This helps the children hone the skills of communicating with their peers peacefully and positively. Usually, the role is designed by the instructor using a particular scenario. Roleplaying is crucial in helping the child think outside the confinement of his immediate environment and be able to function effectively as a team member or leader. This also helps them develop the ability to make independent decisions. The downside of using roleplay as a form of therapy is due to the fact that it is difficult to get everyone to participate in the activities. Therefore, it's imperative to make the scenario as interesting as possible, and if possible, rewards should be provided for the most active group during the roleplay session.

An example of roleplaying can be seen with Danielle, a five years old child of Mrs. Julie. Danielle walked into the classroom a bit uninterested in the class activities as she remembered that she forgot one of her toys at home when they were already halfway to her school. Therefore, Danielle was a bit grumpy and unreceptive. The way she frowned her face indicated that something was wrong. However, Miss. Ross was quite busy enquiring what happened. The child next to Danielle also observed her attitude and teased Danielle with her other friends. They called Danielle several names. It was when they said she looked like a burnt turkey that she got offended, then she shoved the closest child to her and then burst out crying.

The class was disrupted as a result of the clash. However, the teacher was able to contain the conflict and immediately sent them to their respective guidance counselor. Danielle got to the guardian counselor's office, still crying. On arrival, the counselor watched her express her emotions. She wiped her tears with the tissue paper that the counselor provides. Just immediately after crying, she said in a cranky tone, "they did have to do that" why won't people just mind their business?. I was only moody because I forgot my toys at home, then they suddenly started teasing me and calling me all sorts of names. The counselor allowed her to express herself succinctly. Validated her emotions. The counselor told Danielle that she is the CEO of her life and that what people think of her didn't matter at all. Danielle left the counselor's office feeling happy and good. When the counselor saw that Miss. Danielle was already calm, he then made her take action as in a roleplay using the scenario that has just happened. She learned two things for sure; that it doesn't feel good to say harsh words to other people; finally, that it doesn't matter what people said of her. That she is the CEO of her life. Those realizations didn't happen at a spot. This happened after recurrent meetings between Miss Danielle and the guardian counselor. Roleplay makes important life's hack stick to our brain and improves our response when related events occur again. The counselor also videotaped the sessions. Whenever Ms. Danielle goes through the videos, he often bursts into laughter as she assumes how childish she has behaved in the class and never wanted to repeat such an activity.

In conclusion, Social skills are essential skills for every child who wants to enjoy positive peer impact. Loneliness is not an option for any child. Children with ADHD have difficulties paying attention in a group discourse, or if they are intrigued by the discourse, it's hard to take their minds off that. This could interfere with the flow of information. This is particularly hard for people with ADHD. However, these skills can be learned. It requires practice and positive or constructive feedback from the parent, teachers, and close friends. The teachers and the parent have a great role to play in helping the child hone his or her social skills. Social skills come in handy in building and sustaining relationships. Roleplay helps the child develop the ability to delay gratification. It helps develop confidence. Again, feedback plays an important role in helping the child become socially competent. Children with ADHD don't know how their behaviors impact others. Therefore, the parent should always look out for how the child's behavior impacts others and consistently make corrections and expectations. The knowledge of oneself and how others react to their environment is instrumental in building a long-lasting friendship.

3.5 Practices to Improve Listening Skills

In this chapter, we'll go into detail on everything you need to know about improving listening skills in your children, especially those with ADHD.

You might have already noticed that kids tend to tune out of the conversation or selectively decided what they want to hear. This is usually more observable when it relates to things they don't like to hear. For example, asking your kids to do their chores or preventing them from playing video games. When you ask your kids to stop doing things they enjoy doing, they are likely to pretend not to hear anything you say.

It is totally a normal thing for kids to exhibit these behaviors. However, it becomes a huge concern when it occurs repeatedly. If this is the case, then something may be wrong, and you'll need to find a solution to that. Could it be more than just pretending not to be listening? What if your child is actually finding it hard to fully understand what you are saying?

Whichever the case may be, the good news is that listening skills can be improved. As you read on, you'll learn more about listening skills and how you can improve your child's listening skills.

3.5.1   Listening Skills Explained

There's a very thin line between hearing and listening, and many people usually confuse the two. Listening is more about comprehension and how well your child is able to bring out the meaning from every word they hear. The ultimate aim is to be able to relate to what is being said. Ever wondered how kids can hear a story, understand it and narrate it in their words? It's because they were actually listening. In general, listening is a skill that should be developed right from childhood. Remember that a good listener will always be a good communicator.

3.5.2   Why Poor Listening is Bad

Listening is an important skill for communication, and it can significantly impact your child, especially the quality and effectiveness of their relationships with others.

Here are some ways by which a poor listening skill can affect your child negatively:

3.5.2.1   Difficulty Making Friends

A poor listening skill can affect your child's ability to play with their peers. This is because they get distracted easily, and this can affect their quality of play. Also, their higher distractibility can make it harder for them to work in groups or even enjoy some of the associated benefits that come with playing in groups.

3.5.2.2   Sound Awareness Problems

The ability to differentiate sound is also affected by poor listening skills. Sound awareness is also known as phonological awareness, and it's the factor responsible for a child's ability to recognize, identify and work with a different sound.

It is important for kids to be able to know sound elements like tone and loudness. With this, they will be able to differentiate between a happy voice and an angry voice. Another way it can affect kids is that they usually find it hard to understand directions and questions. In some cases, kids with phonological awareness problems can find it hard to understand, follow and complete tasks, and this can lead to behavior problems and low self-esteem.

3.5.2.3 Academic Problems

Listening skills can affect every aspect of a child's life. With poor listening skills, learning becomes hard. Students spend most of their day paying attention to what their teacher has to say. A good listening skill is important for a child to improve their reading ability, grammar, and vocabulary. However, all this cannot be possible if a child has poor listening skills. Communication is not the only thing that's affected. You'll realize that reading becomes harder with poor listening skills.

3.5.3   Characteristics of a Good Listener

Do you have any doubts about whether or not your children are attentive listeners? Your children will need to learn to concentrate all their attention on what they hear to be excellent listeners. They must also know how to identify the critical aspects of the material. To achieve appropriate comprehension, both the listener and the speaker must be engaged.

As parents, it is your responsibility to ensure that your child develops good listening skills, and you can do this by helping them grow into active listeners. You can also help your kids learn to identify key parts of conversations and also ask questions.

Before you try to improve your child's listening skills, you need to set a good example, and here's how to do that:

·   **Prepare yourself for listening:** Unlike adults, children spend more time choosing the right words to use. This is why they often add unnecessary details to conversations. However, as parents, it is important that you exercise patience and hear all they have to say.

· **Being attentive and interested:** Paying attention to your child is important. Kids can know if you're listening or not. When they talk to you, you can try to stop speaking, keep your phone away, or do anything to show that they have your attention.

· **Ask questions:** As you read stories to your kids, always ask them questions, and present them as conversation starters. Questions show interest, and it is important to listen as they answer your questions.

· **Hear them out:** Never cut your child off while they are talking. You might want to correct them, but you should learn to wait till they are done talking.

· **Non-verbal communication:** Facial expressions, posture, energy levels, tone of voice, and behavior pass different messages. Paying attention to these non-verbal signs will help you get hidden messages when your kids talk to you.

· **Encourage talking:** Sometimes, you might need to invite your kids to talk or encourage them to speak up and share their ideas, feelings, and thoughts.

These are the key characteristics of a good listener, and you need to be a good listener before you try to improve your child's listening skills.

3.5.4   Active vs. Passive Listening

As we have mentioned earlier, your child's listening skills play a key role in their day-to-day activities, especially at school. The two main listening skills are passive and active listening.

3.5.4.1 Active Listening

These listening skills involve giving all your attention and ensuring that you fully understand the message being passed on. When listening actively, you're paying attention to every detail, including body language.

3.5.4.1.1 Importance of Active Listening

Here are the benefits of being an active listener:

- More independence

- Fewer misunderstandings

- Improved resourcefulness

- Improved productivity

3.5.4.2 Passive Listening

This is nothing more than hearing what is being said. A passive listener is not concerned about understanding what the speaker is saying. Everyone can voluntarily decide to listen passively, but this shouldn't be a regular thing because it can greatly alter communication.

3.5.5 Your Role as a Parent in Developing Your Child's Listening Skills

Teachers at school usually try their best to develop children's listening skills. However, the remaining part of the job is left to the parents. When trying to improve your child's listening skills, one of the effective things to do is to eliminate negative cycles that might develop as a result of a child being a poor listener. When you notice your child is not listening to what you are saying, try to avoid reacting negatively because doing that will only negatively reward their inattention. Always try to focus on rewarding good behavior. For example, you can reward a child with praises whenever they complete a task because that's a sign that they paid attention to the instructions you gave. Dealing with a child that's not a good listener can be daunting, but with patience, it's easy to achieve.

3.5.6   How to Nurture Good Listening Skills in your Kids

As a parent, one of the essential things you should do regularly is to spend time with your kids. Interact with them regularly, and try to make it fun and interesting. Always try to seize every opportunity to listen to music, read or even sing to your child. You'll be surprised at the impact these little acts will have on their lives. You can also work on developing your child's auditory memory by learning rhymes and songs. When you listen to stories with your kids, you are helping them build their attention stamina.

There are so many activities that you could utilize to improve your child's listening skills. With little effort, you can help nurture their active listening skills.

Here are some of the interesting activities that you could engage in:

- **Identify sounds:** Ask your kids to close their eyes, and then play or make any sound and ask them to identify each sound.

- **Audio stories:** There are many stories that you can use to improve your child's listening skills. You can decide to listen to these stories with your kids and then ask them questions when you are done. With this, they'll always want to pay attention so that they can correctly answer the questions you ask.

- **Add-on stories:** This is more of a good activity in which each participant adds to the story after five sentences

- **Read stories to them:** You can read stories to your kids but also ensure that they are paying attention to it. To make it interactive, you can ask for their thoughts or opinions about the story, or even as them to predict the end of the story.

- **Games:** With games, you can teach your kids how to pay attention to details and follow instructions. You can also use repetition games. For example, saying something and asking your child to repeat what you said. You can also play games like clapping a pattern, broken telephone, or any other copycat game.

One amazing thing is that these things are very easy to do, and what's more is that they are all effective. You can use them to significantly improve your child's listening skills.

3.5.7 How to know that your child has a poor listening skill

As parents, knowing how to improve and nurture your child's listening skills is very important, but you also need to be able to identify when your child has poor listening skills. There are so many signals that you can use to know whether your child is struggling with attention or listening skills.

Here are some signs that can help you know that your child has a problem with listening comprehension:

·   You notice that your child is unable to remember details, especially of what is heard, even though it was recently said.

·   Difficulty learning nursery rhymes and songs

·   Unable to follow conversations

·   You notice that your child is unable to comprehend mathematical words

·   Difficulty spelling and reading, both of which can make the child unable to understand sounds.

·   Your child is easily distracted, especially whenever there's a noise in the background, whether it's a loud noise or not.

·   You notice that your child is always quick to ask for a repetition of what has been said

·   Unable to follow spoken directions, especially if it involves multiple steps.

Listening problem is a completely normal thing with kids, whether the child has ADHD or not. Some kids eventually outgrow this problem, while kids with ADHD find it a lot harder to overcome. Whether your child has ADHD or not, it is your duty as a parent to improve their listening skills.

3.6 How to Be a Positive Parent and Manage the ADHD Effects on your Relationship (Marriage)

The truth is that no one plans to have a child with ADHD or prepare for this journey. We dream of an easy and smooth life when we think of our life as a parent and relationship with a spouse, so it might be overwhelming to discover that your child has ADHD.

The demands of a child with ADHD can affect your mental health and affect the whole family. There would be times when you would get frustrated and then guilt trip yourself for feeling that way.

Remember that there is no perfect parent, and we would all make mistakes in the journey, but how can you be a positive parent finding out that your child has ADHD

One of the most important things you must realize is that this condition is not a death sentence. Your child may not be able to concentrate as easily as other children, but it doesn't mean they won't grow up to succeed in their careers. Children with ADHD can grow up to succeed in a variety of careers. Here are some tips that can help you become a positive parent

3.6.1 Believe in yourself

The first thing to becoming a positive parent is to believe in yourself and be strong. It might be overwhelming, yes, but you have got this. Reaffirm to yourself every day how you are so strong, and you are crushing this. Don't let ADHD get the best of you; rather, be in control of how you feel and react. When you believe that you can do this, the rest is easy.

3.6.2   Believe in your child

Your child may have ADHD, but they have their strengths and trust that your child can learn, change, mature, and succeed.

3.6.3   Take time out

You might need to take breaks because it could be quite exhausting and challenging. Get babysitters so you can sit with friends and relax. Nobody has it all under control.

3.6.4   Join communities and seek support

Most times, you need people to hold your hands and know that you are not alone in this journey. Talk to people who have the same situation as you, join communities in your locality, talk to therapists, and be surprised at how much peace and ease you will feel.

3.6.5   Allow flexibility

You might want to be flexible with your rules as a parent with a child that needs special care. It's important to have rules as they help maintain order, but you might want to consider that children with ADHD find it hard to pay attention to details and require constant reminders.

ADHD can also affect the relationships of the parents because it might be quite overwhelming, especially when there is no proper knowledge of your child's situation. The situation might get rough for the spouse and begin to affect their marriage.

Many couples start blaming each other because it's easier to put the blame on another person rather than yourself, right? It's not an easy battle, and sometimes we feel that we are the only ones feeling the frustration, so we lash out to the nearest person, which in this case can be our partner.

Disagreement may happen when one parent feels left out of a new role; in this instance, you have a kid to care for, but your partner is also preoccupied with assisting the child. When things start to go wrong in the marriage, they spiral out of control, and divorce follows.

The child's treatment could also be a problem, in an instance where a parent feels allowing a child with ADHD to be on his phone for a long period of time could help him make friends and associate with people on social media. Another parent could be of the opinion that it could increase their screen time and inability to focus. This could lead to a dispute in the marriage and separation.

As parents with a child or children with ADHD, how can you achieve a happy home?

3.6.6   Present a united front

After all, if you both agree on matters impacting your kid, many things will become a lot simpler. In this way, improving children's conduct not only benefits their parents; it also alleviates their parents' stress, making them more confident as parents.

3.6.7 Create time to spend quality time together

It's very easy to forget why you both decided to spend the rest of your life together in the first place, and when the purpose is forgotten, abuse is inevitable. It is important to provide room for your marriage so that it may grow. Put your parental responsibilities on hold and be yourself. Helping you discover additional reasons to love and care for each other will enhance our feelings for each other.

3.6.8 Compromise for each other

The truth is that both of you won't always be on the same page on many things, and it might cause rift and disagreement, but when you can compromise and meet in the middle, no one feels left out and misunderstood. It helps the both of you to do things together and help you love each other.

3.6.9 Complement each other

Whenever one parent is going out of their way to do things for the marriage or the children with ADHD, make them feel that you love and appreciate them. This will help me feel that their hard work is not going unnoticed.

3.6.10 Couples therapy

Most people feel they only need therapy when there is a serious rift or misunderstanding, but sometimes all you need is a comfortable environment to have discussions that you might not know how to communicate. It would also help give understanding on how to handle situations that may arise when catering for your child with ADHD.

3.6.11   Be patient

Coming to grips with the diagnosis may take some time. If one of you arrives before your other, allow them time to arrive. You may even need to seek a second opinion. Once you've reached an agreement on the diagnosis, go to work devising your treatment strategies as a team.

It is not easy to raise a kid with ADHD, but some couples report that the experience has strengthened their relationship. To raise a happy, healthy kid, work together. To maintain a solid relationship, do the same.

Thank you for purchasing my book. I have 2 GIFTS FOR YOU: MY audiobook and a free video course regarding "How To Discipline Your Child with ADHD". You can download these materials for free from this link: https://dl.bookfunnel.com/b8yw5x4m7t

3.7   Other Effective Management Options

In the previous chapter of this book, we discussed the pharmacological management of ADHD. Meaning we looked at the various classes of drugs that can be used to manage ADHD and their mechanism of action.

As earlier stated, ADHD has no cure, but it can be managed. Treatment options for ADHD range from medications (stimulants and non-stimulant medications) to behavioral therapy, and use of supplements, and changes in diet. In this chapter, we would be discussing extensively other options that can be used in the management of ADHD.

So Therapeutic ADHD management is inclusive of the following:

- **Psychotherapy**: This management option is useful to get the patients to open up and talk about issues bothering them. It is a form of counseling option for the patient with ADHD to talk about a past incident with their therapist and also to explore their character pattern and enable them to make better choices.

- Psychotherapy also involves Cognitive behavioral therapy (CBT). The goal of CBT is to aid patients with ADHD, especially children focus more on their thoughts, feelings, and characters or behaviors. Generally, CBT helps build self-esteem in patients and treat Anxiety and Depression, which are common in most patients with ADHD.

- **Behavioral Therapy**: The aim of this method of management is to point out negative behaviors and change them to positive ones. In this case, the patient is a child, then the parents of the child, and the counselor all work together to monitor the character pattern and change the negative ones appropriately. Here you develop systems to reward the patient or child when they do things right. This particular management option is perfect for children alongside their medication. Helps them to build their self-esteem and self-control. Parents too should be trained in behavior therapy. This is because for children less than six years of age, the parents undergo training to help them identify character defaults in their children and equip them with strategies to make their children succeed in school, at home, and in their relationships with others. This management option has lasting effects on the patient. We believe that behavioral therapy can equip children with skills that will be useful to them as they grow.

- **Social Skills Training**: If your child or your patients generally are showing signs of difficulty relating in a social environment, then social skills training is needed. In teaching patients new and acceptable behavior, social skills training aims to assist them (or if it is a kid) in developing new behaviors. That makes it easier for them to connect to others. For example, patience, Kindness, Sharing toys or other things, Asking for assistance, and Dealing with taunting may be taught by the therapist or by you as a parent.

- **Support Groups**: This is another great way to manage ADHD; here, the patient can connect with others having the same condition. They share experiences, advice and they learn from each other's growth. In fact, they are presented with practical and real-life strategies for them to learn from.

- Experience, they say, is the best teacher. So here, the patient learns from the life experiences of others and how they were able to cope so that when faced with such difficulty, they know what to do and how to cope.

- Support groups are held frequently and are a great source of the community, especially for a patient newly diagnosed with ADHD. These groups offer support and guidance and a wealth of experience, so you don't feel alone.

- **Use of Supplements**: Medications, both the stimulant and non-stimulant medications used in managing ADHD, may cause serious side effects in some patients, especially children. Therefore, the use of dietary supplements in the management of ADHD is also encouraged. There are lots of dietary supplements that can be taken, and these supplements are readily available in the food we eat or in a local drug store around you.

Note that these supplements are used as Adjunct therapy to support the use of medications and other ADHD treatment options and not to replace them. Examples of these dietary supplements include:

- **Zinc**: It has been shown to have an effect on brain health. Zinc can be gotten from food sources just like: Oysters, Red meat, Dairy products, Whole grains, Beans, Poultry. Zinc is also present as a tablet. The drug Zinc is used in patients with zinc deficiency and also to improve symptoms of ADHD.

- **Omega 3 fatty acid**: This drug is also present in food sources like Salmon, Tuna, Halibut, Mackerel. It is important for brain health as it controls how neurotransmitters dopamine and serotonin move in the frontal cortex of your brain. ADHD occurs in patients with a lower concentration of a type of omega 3 called Docosahexaenoic acid, and the drug can be taken alongside vitamin C for maximum impact.

- **Iron**: This drug should be used in moderation because high levels of iron in the body are not advisable in patients with ADHD. Iron supplements help to increase the production of neurotransmitters in the brain. This, in turn, improves mood, regulates emotions, regulates stress, and regulates the brain's reward system.

- **Magnesium**: This supplement is important for mental health but only in cases where patients are magnesium deficient. If the patient is not magnesium deficient, then there is no need for the drug. Magnesium can also be gotten in food like Dairy products, Whole grains, Beans, Leafy vegetables. Magnesium works by improving mood, reducing irritability, mental confusion, and shortened attention span.

- **Melatonin**: Melatonin does not directly impact ADHD, but it is useful in regulating sleep, which is a side effect of ADHD.

Herbal remedies can also be used in the management of ADHD also as an adjunct therapy. These help to reduce hyperactivity, impulsive behavior, they increase attention span, lack of sleep, and social behavior is also improved. The herbal remedies

- Ginkgo Biloba.

- Korean ginseng.

- Valerian root and Lemon balm.

General tips for patients with ADHD to try out include:

- Spending more time outside, this tip benefits children as it helps them to increase their concentration and mood.

- Participate in Yoga classes; this improves all-around symptoms of ADHD and makes the patient more focused, and also increases attention. Studies have shown that patients that undergo yoga have a high attention span and increased concentration.

- Avoid allergens. This helps to increase attention and concentration.

Tips For Managing ADHD as an Adult.

Managing ADHD as an adult seems difficult, but it is very possible. To help you lead a well-meaning and meaningful life as an adult with ADHD, here are a few suggestions to get you started. Keep these strategies in mind:

- For stress management and to boost your mood, spend a lot of time outdoors, and do exercise.

- Get plenty of sleep. Have a sleep-wake schedule and stick to it. Do not take caffeine late in the day.

- Eat healthy by eating smaller portions of food, avoid sugar and junk, eat a protein a day, and meals rich in fiber.

- Be mindful; this helps you reduce impulsivity and increase concentration and attention span. Make Meditation a habit for better focus.

- To increase productivity, always learn to set time for each task and write things down; this helps manage forgetfulness and prioritize by doing more important tasks first.

- For effective time management, assign deadlines to pending tasks, make wearing wristwatches a habit, set reminders.

- For effective prioritization, Do one thing at a time, decide what task you want to do first, stay on task (do not try to juggle more than you can handle). This helps to handle procrastination. Also, learn to say NO, so you don't take up more tasks than you can handle.

Tips For Managing ADHD in Children.

ADHD in children might seem difficult to handle, but it is possible. Having ADHD is not the end of the world, as kids can still live a normal life if detected early and if managed well. Here are tips to help children with ADHD:

- As a parent, set up a reward system for your child if he or she completes a task or behaves in a positive way, or shows improvement.

160

- Have a consistent schedule and routine for your child. Everything from sleeping to waking up to eating all should have a clear routine that should be maintained.

- Using organizers and reminders for your child to stay on track helps to keep them focused.

Attention deficit hyperactivity disorder (ADHD) cannot be cured, but it may be successfully treated to enable the patient have a healthy life. If these tips and strategies discussed in this chapter are affected alongside their medications, that patient is well on their way to live a good life.

4   CONNECTING WITH YOUR CHILD

4.1 Effective Methods to Contrast Behavioral Challenges

From the previous chapters, I've mentioned that kids with ADHD are likely to experience other mental health problems compared to other kids. Different studies have been performed on kids with ADHD, and one such study began with kids with the age of 8 and progressed into adulthood. The results and findings of this study showed that kids with ADHD had a higher chance of behavioral challenges, anxiety, learning differences, substance abuse, self-injury, and depression. The study also showed that during adolescence, there is a higher tendency for a kid with ADHD to develop these issues.

Knowledge is power, and to be able to contrast behavioral challenges, you need to learn about these behaviors, the symptoms that might develop, and how to identify them. With this, you can come up with an effective method to use in taking early actions. What's certain is that doing this will yield a better outcome for you and your child with ADHD.

4.1.1   Behavioral Problems

There are diverse behavioral challenges that can occur in children with ADHD, but the most common is aggressive behavior and defiant. These challenges are usually expressed as refusing to follow instructions or directions from teachers or parents. Children with ADHD, like other people with ADHD, tend to be more rebellious than their peers. They are prone to emotional outbursts, particularly when required to do physically or mentally demanding tasks.

According to Dr. Vasco Lopes, a specialist in disruptive behaviors and ADHD, kids with ADHD are more likely to become defiant in different situations. Examples of these situations include going to bed, completing homework, eating dinner, sitting down, or quitting playtime. In general, kids with ADHD find it difficult to tolerate these situations, and this is mainly due to some deficits associated with ADHD, which also include:

- Controlling activity level

- Reining in impulses

- Transitioning between activities

- Tolerating boring situations

- Paying attention

4.1.2   Understanding when defiance becomes a disorder

How severe is your child's defiance? Do you think it is to a level that can make life difficult for them at home or in school? If this occurs too frequently, then your child may be diagnosed with a disorder, but it would depend on their age and the symptoms they show. Here are some of the diagnoses that may be given after your child has been evaluated:

- **Disruptive mood dysregulation disorder (DMDD):**
This is used in describing when a child is always irritable. For

example, having a severe and frequent temper or emotional outbursts. In most cases, these outbursts tend to be out of proportion. Most kids diagnosed with ADHD are usually diagnosed with DMDD as well.

- **Conduct Disorder (CD):** This occurs when a child is more likely to be disruptive, aggressive, deceitful, and regularly breaking the rules. Most kids with ADHD, especially the combined-type ADHD, have conduct disorder

- **Oppositional Defiance Disorder (ODD):** This is used in describing a child that is hostile, defiant, and uncooperative. ODD is also when a child frequently behaves in annoying ways, and it usually occurs in 50% of kids with combined-type ADHD. Kids with only the inattentive-type ADHD are also likely to have ODD.

4.1.3   Parent Training Strategy

While it's important for parents to be educated on the unique behavioural difficulties faced by kids with ADHD, there are two trainings that may help: Parent-Child Interaction Therapy and Parent Management Training (PCIT). Both trainings have proven to be effective in helping parents and their kids with ADHD, especially when they start to show behavioral challenges like emotional outbursts and defiance.

Here's a brief overview of how this training will help you:

- PMT and PCIT will improve your relationship with your child and also reduce stress

- Both will teach you effective ways to pay attention to the positive behaviors of your child

- The two parent training will help to reduce aggression, disobedient, and disruptiveness behaviors

- Both will teach you how to provide consequences for aggressive behavior and other major misbehaviors.

- Both train you to ignore minor misbehaviors

- PCIT will let you interact with your child and also allow you to learn skills you can use from a therapist through life coaching.

- PMT will teach you skills in the absence of your child

4.1.4   Conditions that accompany ADHD

4.1.4.1   Learning Differences

Difficulty learning to read or math-related learning problems are very common in kids with ADHD. However, it usually depends on the age of the child, and the learning difficulties may be in one of the following areas:

- Following directions

- Making rhymes

- Continuously making the same mistakes even after being corrected over and over again

- Blurting out unfamiliar words

- Associating sounds with symbols

- Confusing simple math symbols

- Sequencing sounds in the correct order

In some cases, learning something new in class may not be a problem for the child, but the problem comes in when they are asked to reproduce or apply what they have learned at home or in a different setting.

Do you think your child has a learning disability?

The Individuals with Disabilities Education Act prompts schools to provide evaluation for kids. With this, an effective treatment plan can be drafted, and this takes into account ways of improving learning skills and coming up with learning strategies centered on the child's strengths.

4.1.4.2 Depression

It is already a known fact that kids with ADHD have a greater chance of developing depression, especially in adolescence. Here are the symptoms to watch out for:

- Withdrawing from others, including family members

- Change in appetite

- Change in sleeping patterns

- Irritability

- Unreasonable fears

- Decline in academic performance

- Loss of interest in almost everything

Here's what you can do if you notice any of these symptoms

If you observe these symptoms for more than a week and they start to interfere with their life at home, in school, or with friends, then you know that it's time to go for an evaluation.

One thing you should note is that treatment for ADHD does not always relieve the symptoms of depression. For kids with depression, cognitive behavioral therapy may be required. When this is combined with antidepressant medications, it can be significantly helpful.

4.1.4.3 Anxiety

This is more common in kids with ADHD, and it can take any of the following forms.

- **Obsessive-compulsive disorder:** When someone is preoccupied with thoughts of dread and sometimes resorts to self-imposed routines to manage them, they are said to be suffering from Obsessive-Compulsive Disorder (OCD).

  - **Social anxiety:** Fear of new situations and new people, such that it affects daily life

  - **Generalized anxiety disorder:** Getting excessively worried about nothing. In kids, it can be a phobia for certain foods, school, germs, and more

  - **Separation anxiety:** Being fearful of being separated from parents, or other family members

If you notice that your child is always worried or scared, or if it begins to interfere with their daily life, whether at home or in school, then you might need to go for an anxiety evaluation. You can also use CBT in combination with medications for anxiety.

4.1.4.4 Substance Abuse

This is very common with teenagers, especially those with ADHD. Kids with ADHD usually have low self-esteem, and this can draw them to other kids with a high tendency to abuse alcohol and other drugs. In general, kids with ADHD have a very high chance of abusing a substance, but the good thing is that when placed on medication, the risk lowers. This is because the medications are effective in controlling impulsive behavior, which is the major factor that can lead to substance abuse.

Always supervise your child's activities, as well as the type of friends they spend time with. Always know where your child is and what they are up to. ADHD kids with parents who supervise their activities have a lower chance of abusing substances. Another strategy is to let your child know that you're always available to talk to them and support them in any way. Kids with a substance abuse problem will need to be isolated for treatment.

4.1.4.5   Self-injury

Also common in teenagers with ADHD, especially teenage girls. They have a higher tendency for self-injury, like cutting. Studies show that about 55% of girls with combined-type ADHD will show varying forms of self-injury. It is also likely to occur in kids with inattentive-type ADHD.

Things to look out for include:

- Adhesive bandages

- Frequently talking about self-injuring

- Refusal to change clothes or go into the locker room

- Avoiding social activities

- Weird scars

- Increased isolation

- Prefers to wear long-sleeved shirts, even in warm weather

- Always in possession of sharp objects

- Cuts in the same spot

If you notice any of the above, try to respond as fast as possible because it can become an addictive habit. When kids continue to inflict harm on themselves, they start to get the urge to do it repeatedly. Try to stop it before they do it repeatedly up to 10 times.

Kids with ADHD are generally more likely to have other mental health and behavioral issues. Fortunately, parents who are aware of the possible issues and those who know how to identify these issues can take early actions in order to prevent the issues from becoming serious. One interesting thing is that the issues usually resolve as the child grows into adulthood.

The best thing is to always know what to look out for and to provide solutions as fast as possible.

4.2 Identifying Your Discipline Philosophy

There are different discipline philosophies, and it is important that you learn them so that you can know which one will work best for your child with ADHD. In this chapter, I'll focus on the different discipline philosophies and provide an effective strategy for your child with ADHD.

One of the toughest and most challenging parts of parenthood is discipline. This can discourage, humble, or frustrate you. Whenever you are faced with these challenges, especially when getting your child, whether a toddler or a big kid, to behave, you might start to get a nostalgic feeling of when they were just babies and how easy it was to handle them.

All you need is to find an ideal philosophy that will match your style. However, you need to know how and when to use these philosophies. The interesting thing is that you can select more than one discipline philosophy and leave the rest. What matters most is that you are using the right philosophy for your child with ADHD.

As you read the different philosophies below, I strongly advise that you pay attention to your feelings while reading each style.

4.2.1   How the discipline theories differ?

There is so much advice from different experts, and when you hear these, it'd only leave you confused and frustrated. For example, while one expert is saying that time-outs will only last a minute, another is saying your child will decide how long a time-out will last. Also, in some books, you'll be advised not to use words like "don't" and "no," while other books will outrightly ask you to use these words when correcting your child. All of these only cause more confusion.

The truth of the matter is that even though these people are experts, and the recommendations will work in some situations, the ultimate expert when it comes to determining what will work for your child is you. Yes, you are the only true expert that can determine the type of discipline to use on your kids. Professional advice is important and helpful, but I always advise parents to merge this with their ideals and intuition.

4.2.2   The Discipline Philosophies

4.2.2.1   Boundary-based discipline

In some instances, a child will only feel safe when there's a boundary. They'll continue to try different things until they can identify where such boundaries exist. A child would want to know what will happen if they throw the key away or use an object to make so much noise. Most kids will want to test limits just to see their parent's reactions

If you're patient, you don't have to wait for them to be inquisitive and decide to push these boundaries. Effective communication is essential here. It is crucial to convey limits to your children as parents. The other thing you can do is have your kid put away toys when they're done with them. You can also attach a consequence for not doing these things rightly, but the consequence should be logical enough.

It's always best to utilize natural consequences. For example, leaving your child to experience a bit of the consequence of forgetting their lunch box at home. Rather than rush to get it to them, you can decide to delay a bit.

4.2.2.2   Gentle Discipline

Children can't learn when they are in tears or screaming. There's so much for you and your child to benefit from when you use daily preventive strategies. This has a higher tendency to reduce the tendency of them to misbehave.

You can create routines that will make your child feel grounded. Give them choices and make them feel a bit of control, and whenever there's a transition, always give them prior notice. For example, when out on the back, you can give them ten minutes' notice before you leave, rather than asking them to leave on the spot.

Ensure that your request to them is always positive. Also try to be strategic with your response to them. For example, when your child asks to go out to play but yet to do homework, you might be tempted to say NO. However, the best thing is to say, "you can go out after completing your homework" There are so many instances where you can apply this strategy, and what's certain is that it's far better than being direct with your answers.

Sometimes, a kid's misbehavior may be a result of hunger, boredom, or tiredness. You need to pay attention to these because once solved; they won't misbehave anymore.

4.2.2.3   Positive Discipline

One way to ensure that your child behaves well all the time is by ensuring that they have a sense of belonging and feel encouraged. Children will always misbehave whenever they feel discouraged. Always communicate with your child, and don't be quick to judge them when they misbehave. Try to find out the cause of their misbehavior.

For example, if your child refuses to wash the dishes rather than should on them, you can try to find out why. Shouting at kids will only instill fear, which is not good. But when you sit your kids down to reason with them, it gives them a sense of belonging, which is perfect for them to behave well. Once you have identified their reason for not doing something, you can then encourage them or find a solution that will help them work better.

The whole idea about positive discipline is utilizing misbehavior and turning it into a learning opportunity for your child.

4.2.2.4 Emotion-coaching

Helping kids understand their feelings will make them make better decisions. Therefore, it is important for parents to teach their kids how to understand their emotions. Doing this will also help you connect with your child.

The first thing you should do is identify your standards and know the things you can accept and things you won't accept. From there, you can now communicate these things with your child and ensure that you let them understand some of the feelings they are likely to get when they experience these things.

Always try to put yourself in their shoes and see what they a feeling. That way, you'll be able to understand why they are misbehaving. This will also help you know the best way to communicate to their feelings with them.

One interesting thing about this philosophy is that it will help you build trust with your kids.

4.2.2.5 Behavior modification

You can alter good and bad behaviors. All you have to do is utilize positive reinforcement to increase good behaviors and negative reinforcement to cause a decline in bad behaviors. You might want to think this approach is similar to the boundary-based discipline philosophy. However, the difference is that behavior modification places more emphasis on rewards and warnings.

With warnings, you can help your child stop misbehaving and teach them to take responsibility for their actions. Sometimes, you might need to give these warnings a couple of times till you achieve your goal. In cases where the offense is rather too serious, you can come up with a consequence that will help them realize that they are misbehaving.

With Rewards, you can motivate your child. It doesn't have to be something extravagant, and as simple as parental praise can do the job. As parents, always try to reward your child when they behave well.

These are the different discipline philosophies, and one thing about them is that they overlap each other. Now that you know these philosophies, we can move on to strategies that will help you.

4.2.3   Discipline Strategies for an ADHD Child

Disciplining a child with ADHD can be an arduous task, and you might need different approaches to be able to achieve this. With a few parenting strategies, you can easily help your child manage their behavior.

Here are some discipline strategies that I would recommend:

4.2.3.1 Provide Positive Attention

It is exhausting to parent a kid with ADHD, but you cannot refuse to have children with ADHD since it's part of their condition. While having ADHD, kids will always have an intense urge to keep talking. Additionally, their energy levels are on the high side, and you may be worn out in the long term. As always, the best gift you can give your kid is your attention. No matter how busy your schedule will ever get, always try to devote time (even if it's just 15 minutes) for your kids.

4.2.3.2 Praise their Efforts

Do not hesitate to congratulate your kid whenever you observe them doing anything nice. Praises will motivate kids, especially kids with ADHD. Therefore, try to praise them frequently. When praising your kids, also try to ensure that it is as specific as it can be.

4.2.3.3 Give Effective Instructions

For a child with a short attention span, you'll need to be careful when giving them instructions. Also, they may require further assistance following these instructions. In some cases, these kids don't hear what is said the first time and may need you to repeat yourself.

Before giving any instruction to your child, always try to get their full attention. You can eliminate every form of distraction, like turning off the television and maintaining eye contact with them. The bottom line is that you should always have their full attention before you make any request.

Chain commands are very common, but this is something you might want to avoid, especially with an ADHD child. This is because they may not be able to follow through to the last command. Therefore, with ADHD kids, always give one instruction at a time.

4.2.3.4 Ignore Mild Misbehaviors

Attention-seeking behavior is a very common thing with ADHD kids. That is why it is important that you always give them all the attention they want. While doing this, you are likely to observe some mild misbehaviors. You don't have to always point these misbehaviors out. Sometimes they are just to get your attention, and when you ignore them for a while, they will stop these misbehaviors with time.

4.2.3.5 Use Time-Out When Necessary

This is an effective way to help your ADHD child calm their brains and bodies. Time-out doesn't mean harsh punishment, but it's a life skill that will come in handy in many situations. Let your kids know the importance of going to a quiet place and staying quiet for a period, especially whenever they are frustrated or overstimulated.

When doing this, try to ensure that they don't get the idea that you're punishing them for misbehaving. With time, your child will learn how to go to quiet places when they are hyperactive.

4.2.3.6 Use Natural Consequences

I've mentioned this earlier but will reiterate it further. Disciplining a child with ADHD requires that you act wisely. When doing this, always ensure that your child does not start to think they don't get anything right. Sometimes, when you let some behaviors slide, you are helping yourself and your child.

In many cases, natural consequences have a way of teaching kids not to repeat some things they did in the past. You don't have to force a child to eat breakfast before going to school. Allow their wish prevail, and watch the results. In this case, hunger is the natural consequence.

4.2.3.7 Work with their Teacher

Working with your child's teacher will help to increase their success in school. Sometimes a child with ADHD will require specific school work modifications like extending test time.

You might also need to include behavioral modifications sometimes. When doing this, it is advisable to ensure that it's one both at home and in school.

4.2.3.8 Reward Systems

This is a great and effective way to make your child maintain focus on what they do. However, using the conventional reward system in which a child will have to wait long to get can only bore a child with ADHD. Sometimes you might need to use a token-based system in which your child will earn throughout the day. Rewards will come in handy in teaching your child to do things right, and they will also help them stay motivated and focused on what they do.

4.3 Mastering Effective Communication Methods

One of the challenges that come with parenting a child with ADHD is communication. Upon interacting with different parents with an ADHD child, I've come to realize that most of these parents sometimes find it hard to communicate with their kids. Sometimes, they do not know the best way to make their kids understand simple things, and this can be frustrating. In some cases, they do not know how to get their kids to follow directions, slow down, or pay attention to important things. The communication problem becomes worse if the parent has ADHD.

As a parent, one thing you should understand is that the mind of kids with ADHD is always busy. It's safe to imagine their brain as a very busy city, with different information, sensory input, impulses, directions, and many other distractions. However, in this city of theirs, there are no traffic lights, and this only causes chaos and confusion.

Maintaining effective communication with your child is very important. It is what will determine if your directions are clear enough. Also, when communicating with your kids, always try to give them choices and break tasks into smaller units. Rather than making statements, you can decide to ask questions. Doing this will force your kids to think of possible alternatives.

You need to understand that for a child with ADHD, and you'll require more than just talking to communicate with them. These kids are special, and if you are not careful, you'll only talk until your face turns blue, and the child still doesn't get what you're trying to say.

Most parents don't usually know how to handle temper tantrums which are likely to occur frequently in a child with ADHD, especially if they are frustrated or having an emotional outburst. It is also beneficial for parents to view these temper outbursts as a chance to demonstrate their honesty. To succeed, you must convey to your kid that their tantrums will not and cannot harm you.

Staying cool is one of the most effective methods to soothe a kid with these regular tantrums. You should notice emotional outbursts or meltdowns in your kid; therefore, you should attempt to remain calm and observe the situation. The best way to demonstrate to your kid that you are the adult in their life and that you have everything under control is to provide stability confidently. It is important for your child to see you as an emotionally strong person who can handle their tantrums, no matter how severe they may be.

Your child might already be used to seeing you getting upset whenever they show these tantrums. Therefore, trying something new will freak them out. Imagine if your child is at it again, and rather than raising your voice or losing it, you sit down, drink water or do something different to stay calm. This will hit your child by surprise, and they'll also be forced to calm down. Once they are calm, you can proceed to invite them to your space and talk to them.

When you do this, you are helping your child understand that you are emotionally strong, and soon, you'll become their hero.

Whether your child has ADHD or not, communicating with them is very important. For kids with ADHD or any other attention issue, communication can be hard, and this can lead to misunderstandings in different ways.

Here are strategies that you can use to strengthen communication with your child:

· **Explain your expectations:** Attempt to make time to explain things to your children as plainly as possible. This ensures that they have a clear idea of what is expected of them and what is to be avoided. Teaching youngsters that they know what is expected of them and what they may anticipate in return will positively affect their behavior. You can also support this strategy by using rewards for positive behaviors.

· **Remain calm and talk softly:** It's normal to feel agitated or want to raise your voice. However, always remember that this will only stimulate your child. Always try to stay calm, and speak quietly whenever your child is upset. You can also step away whenever they start to throw tantrums. I recommend anything quiet activity during this time, rather than raising your voice at them.

· **Visual aids:** Visual aids have proven to be effective for kids with ADHD, and you might want to consider using them. You can use these visual aids to communicate effectively with your kids. Rather than telling them what to do, you can make representations of these things on posters and show them to your child with ADHD.

· **Choices:** Whenever a child notices that you are talking at them and not to them, they are likely to tune you out. However, giving them choices will make it a lot easier for them to pay attention to what you're saying. This is because they will analyze both options and see which one suits them more. For example, when you ask your child to wear their pajamas, they are likely to ignore it for one reason or the other. However, when you say, "would you like to wear the blue pajamas or the yellow one," your child would think and choose one.

· **Create communication strategies:** Communicating to a child with ADHD will require that you apply creative measures. It's not an easy journey, which is why you'll need a very high level of patience. Be open to trying different communication strategies until you have found one that works fine for you and your child.

· **Give simple and short directions:** Kids get overwhelmed easily, and it's even more when the child has ADHD. Always give step-by-step instructions whenever you want a child with ADHD to perform a task. However, you'll need to be careful when giving these instructions. Try to avoid giving all the steps at once, because they are likely to forget everything. Give them a few instructions first, and then wait for them to complete them before proceeding to the next steps.

Recognize when your child is paying attention or simply hearing you: The mind of kids with ADHD is always operating at a very fast pace. Therefore, you cannot always expect them to maintain eye contact with you, and this doesn't mean that they are not listening to you. You'd be surprised to know that they are listening even though they are playing with another object. Whenever you are talking to your child with ADHD, always pay attention to their every move, and find cues that will suggest whether they are listening or not.

4.4   A peaceful connexion

It is not just enough to say you love and care for your child. Everybody can talk, but what are you doing to show that you love and care for them? The way you care for a child with ADHD is totally different from how you care for others. It is easy to have it all planned out in your head but are you caring and connecting with your child the right way?

Loving and connecting with children with ADHD can seem impossible due to the effects of the disorder, but the fact remains that all children with ADHD or not deserve love and affection. The process might seem impossible, but it's achievable. Here are some steps to help you connect with your child

Below are some tips that will help you connect with your child with ADHD. Read on!

4.4.1   Be ready to put in the work

To make anything work, you must be ready to put your strength and energy into it, and this also works with connecting with your child. You must be ready to go out of your comfort zone and shake yourself up a little. You would often feel like giving up or just throwing in the towel but remember that you have a child that needs your care and support.

4.4.2   Create a comfortable atmosphere for the child

When the environment is comfortable and serene for both the child and the parent, things will flow naturally. When a child feels comfortable in an environment, it is easy for the child to open up to the parent about what he is going through, but when the environment is filled with fear, you would not know or understand how the child is feeling and how you can come in as a parent.

4.4.3   Build trust with your child

A popular adage says that trust is earned and not demanded. As a parent, it is easy to demand trust because you feel it is your right instead of forcing trust on the child. Trust could mean delivering your promise to them; if you know you would not be able to keep to your promise, do not make them.

Trust could also mean showing up no matter what. If you are to pick your child from school at the said time, DO IT. If you know you want to attend a baseball game they are playing in, SHOW UP. This helps build and fosters trust.

4.4.4   Do not hold hurt against them

For children with ADHD, it is normal for them to forget instructions you give them because they find it hard to concentrate, but you must remember that they are not doing intentionally, and sometimes we could get really mad at them for not meeting up with tasks and deadlines, but you always have to let go. Do not hold these issues against you or affect the relationship you have with them.

4.4.5   Create healthy communication

You must pay attention to your children and their unvoiced desires and feelings. Instead of ignoring people, please pay attention to them and speak to them freely about subjects you usually wouldn't. By rejecting your kid as soon as they talk to you, you lose out on learning about and teaching your child, and she comes to understand that you aren't attentive, which makes communication pointless.

4.4.6   Use the right disciplinary measures

To discipline your children with a long-term solution, you must resort to spanking. But, on the other hand, spanking has the benefit of providing parents with short-term compliance.

But this approach is ineffective in teaching children about right and wrong. Instead, it simply encourages the kid to dread repercussions outside of the situation. Then the kid fears being caught, which motivates him to avoid it.

There are statistics that show that children who are spanked or flogged are prone to fighting and may likely become bullies.

Other ways to correct your child include:

Mete out consequences

Reassure your kid that their actions will result in consequences, including taking away privileges or restricting their activities. However, it's important that you do not take away things that your child needs.

Give them the chance to explain

As we have stated earlier, listen to your child and pay close attention to what they say. You would be surprised at the things you would learn and be able to solve. Talk to your child rather than lashing out every time.

You don't have to respond to everything

Responding to every mistake your child makes would end up frustrating you and your child because they will likely feel that they never get everything right. There are many things you should overlook for your mental health, don't get me wrong, your child needs to be corrected, but when you can turn a blind eye to a mistake, it is advisable that you should

Set rules

It is very important to set rules for your children, so they know what is expected of them. For children with ADHD, they might need constant reminders on what is expected of them. Rather than being quick to spank your child, take out time to explain what you need them to do.

Parenting a child with ADHD might be different from what we all know. Home customs and traditions could be difficult to inculcate in your child. Creating family traditions could be impossible depending on how severe the effects of ADHD.

Realizing that your children with ADHD are structured differently than other children. While children have to make extra efforts to understand what is acceptable and what is not, they still have a problem with understanding and assimilating. Even at that, they might still not get it right.

Although the symptoms of ADHD could be very frustrating to deal with as a parent, always try and reaffirm that your child who is ignoring, annoying, or embarrassing you is not doing so intentionally. Your child wants to make you happy, obey instructions, and be organized, but they really can't help themselves.

You have to learn to manage your child's behavior and seek treatments and medications, which is a very important step in the journey of your child. You must understand that it's not easy for your child, just as it is for you. With care, love, and unwavering support, you and your child can have an easy journey that would make a very home.

Download the Audio Book Version of This Book for FREE

If you love listening to audio books on-the-go, I have great news for you. You can download the audio book version of this book for **FREE** just by signing up for a **FREE** 30-day Audible trial! See below for more details!

As an audible customer, you will receive the below benefits with your 30-day free trial:

- FREE audible book copy of this book
- After the trial, you will get 1 credit each month to use on any audiobook
- Your credits automatically roll over to the next month if you don't use them
- Choose from Audible's 200,000 + titles
- Listen anywhere with the Audible app across multiple devices
- Make easy, no-hassle exchanges of any audiobook you don't love
- Keep your audiobooks forever, even if you cancel your membership

Click the links below to get started!

For Audible US
https://www.audible.com/pd/B09NNS88XD/?source_code=AUDFPWS0223189MWT-BK-ACX0-290151&ref=acx_bty_BK_ACX0_290151_rh_us

For Audible UK
https://www.audible.co.uk/pd/B09NNR39Z9/?source_code=AUKFrDlWS02231890H6-BK-ACX0-290151&ref=acx_bty_BK_ACX0_290151_rh_uk

For Audible FR:
https://www.audible.fr/pd/B09NNSXS58/?source_code=FRAORWS022318903B-BK-ACX0-290151&ref=acx_bty_BK_ACX0_290151_rh_fr

For Audible DE
https://www.audible.de/pd/B09NNSSQ1T/?source_code=EKAORWS0223189009-BK-ACX0-290151&ref=acx_bty_BK_ACX0_290151_rh_de

5   CONCLUSION

ADHD is a completely manageable disorder that's common in children and adults. Managing a child with ADHD can be an arduous task, and if care is not taken, parents might lose it, ignore the child's condition, which can even make matters worse. In most cases, ADHD usually occurs alongside other issues like anxiety and depression, all of which are completely manageable.

Parenting kids with ADHD is not as easy as it may sound, especially for parents who equally have the condition. The first thing you should do as a parent is to understand everything about the condition. Fortunately, this book has covered all the key aspects of ADHD, and even more. With this, you have all the information you need, and the only thing left will be to start applying this information in managing your child's condition.

In the first part of this book, I covered the medical aspect of ADHD, where I talked about the ADHD, and treatment used, particularly drug therapy. There are so many drug treatment options for use in children with ADHD, including stimulants and non-stimulants. However, this information is not provided so that you become your child's prescriber. Always consult a physician before giving your child any medication. One amazing thing about the medication is that they are all effective, and the results obtained are encouraging, especially when combined with regular medication.

In the second part of the book, I moved on to provide information that can further help you to understand your child's condition. It is when you understand the condition that you'll be able to come up with effective strategies to handle the condition. I also provided tips to help you navigate through tantrums.

The third part of the book centered on managing your child's condition with methods other than the use of drugs, while the fourth chapter focused on providing ways to help parents connect with their children. With all of this, you can comfortably manage your child's ADHD condition and prevent it from affecting their day-to-day activities.

Raising a kid with ADHD comes with its own set of unique difficulties. However, as a parent of a kid with ADHD, you should never forget that there are no shortcuts to learning. This is mainly because ADHD expresses itself with different symptoms and degrees of severity. With a tailor-made or person-centered approach, your child will enjoy great benefits.

Poor impulse control leading to inappropriate and challenging behaviors is a common symptom of ADHD. However, the first step for every parent is to accept their child's condition and come to terms with the fact that ADHD is nothing more than a functional difference in the brain of their kids. Also, having a child with ADHD doesn't mean that child will not be able to learn to distinguish right from wrong. There are so many ways to support and help an ADHD child to develop all the positive behavior.

Another important thing is for caregivers and parents to find their own way to interact with these kids. This includes gestures, physical environment, emotional language and speech. In order to manage ADHD effectively, consistency is the most essential. Using structured and supportive approaches can significantly help in reducing challenging behaviors and help the child excel.

There are so many ongoing research into ADHD. New and effective ways of living with the condition are tested regularly, and this includes sociological, psychological and medical ways. Unlike a few decades back, ADHD has more social acceptance which is a great thing for managing the condition. This also helps in providing support for parents and caregivers of kids with ADHD.

Interacting with ADHD kids requires much care. In general, these kids are usually first diagnosed with ADHD when they are 7 years which is a very young age. Keeping a conversation with a normal 7 year old child can be difficult and it even becomes more difficult with an ADHD child. However, even though these difficulties may present, it is important to speak to the child regularly because this can benefit both the parent and the child.

Always try to use age-appropriate languages when conversing with these kids. Remember that you do not want to give unnecessary details before achieving your goal. Also, with more conversations about ADHD, the child's curiosity about their condition also increases. With that in mind, here are statements that can help you start a conversation with an ADHD child:

- **ADHD is not a flaw:** Help the child understand that their condition is not bad, neither is it a flaw, or a weakness. It doesn't make other kids better than they are, and it is like every other condition that when supported rightly, it won't affect the person's life negatively.

- **ADHD has no effect on intelligence:** An ADHD child can be as smart as every other child can be. When you talk to your kids, always try to remind them that there are so many great thinkers that had ADHD right from when they were kids. An example is Thomas Edison and Albert Einstein

- **You can succeed in life, even with ADHD:** You can do this by providing your child with positive role models, particularly people who have succeeded with the condition. There are so many celebrities that have had to deal with ADHD, including Solange Knowles, and Will Smith. Allow you child to admire these people and let them be their motivation.

Even though having a child with ADHD requires so much thinking and planning, the whole process becomes fulfilling and pleasurable, especially when you get the desired results you want.

Thank you for purchasing my book. I have 2 GIFTS FOR YOU: MY audiobook and a free video course regarding "How To Discipline Your Child with ADHD". You can download these materials for free from this link: https://dl.bookfunnel.com/b8yw5x4m7t

6 REFERENCES

- American Psychiatric Association. (2013). Diagnostic and statistical manual of mental disorders (5th ed.). Arlington, VA: Author.

- Siegel, D. J., & Bryson, T. P. (2016). No-drama discipline: the whole-brain way to calm the chaos and nurture your child's developing mind. Trade Paperback Edition. New York: Bantam Books.

- Siegel, D. J., & Bryson, P. H. D. T. P. (2012). The whole-brain child. Random House.

- www.worldwidescience.org/topicpages/d/disorders+attention+deficit.html

- Ian P Stolerman (2010), Encyclopedia of Psychopharmacology, Springer

- www.additudemag.com/what-is-adhd-symptoms-causes-treatments/

- Mengühan Araz Altay, Işık Görker, Begüm Demirci Şipka, Leyla Bozatlı, Tuğçe Ataş (2020), Attention Deficit Hyperactivity Disorder and Psychiatric Comorbidities, Euras J Fam Med

- www.blogarama.com/health-and-fitness-blogs/1295402-healthinfi-secure-health-blog/23895434-about-addadhd

- Harris R. Lieberman (2007) Cognitive methods for assessing mental energy, Nutritional Neuroscience, 10:5-6, 229-242, DOI: 10.1080/10284150701722273

- Balbinot P, Testino G (2020) The Introduction of Self Help Group Facilitator in an Alcohol Unit: Preliminary Results. Int Arch Subst Abuse Rehabil 2:008. doi.org/10.23937/2690-263X/1710008

- www.ninds.nih.gov/disorders/patient-caregiver-education/fact-sheets/tourette-syndrome-fact-sheet

- Practitioner Review : Current best practice in the use of parent training and other behavioural interventions in the treatment of children and adolescents with attention deficit hyperactivity disorder. / Daley, David; Van Der Oord, Saskia; Ferrin, Maite; Cortese, Samuele; Danckaerts, Marina; Doepfner, Manfred; Van den Hoofdakker, Barbara J; Coghill, David; Thompson, Margaret; Asherson, Philip; Banaschewski, Tobias; Brandeis, Daniel; Buitelaar, Jan; Dittmann, Ralf W; Hollis, Chris; Holtmann, Martin; Konofal, Eric; Lecendreux, Michel; Rothenberger, Aribert; Santosh, Paramala; Simonoff, Emily; Soutullo, Cesar; Steinhausen, Hans Christoph; Stringaris, Argyris; Taylor, Eric; Wong, Ian C K; Zuddas, Alessandro; Sonuga-Barke, Edmund J. In: Journal of Child Psychology and Psychiatry, 30.10.2017.

- www.churchillstl.org/learning-disability-resources/adhd/

- www.fiercebiotech.com/biotech/head-to-head-study-demonstrates-focalin-r-xr-offers-faster-and-better-symptom-control-than

- EAPC Abstracts. Palliative Medicine. 2019;33(1):118-589. doi:10.1177/0269216319844405

- When Your Child's ADHD Affects You as a Couple. https://www.webmd.com/add-adhd/childhood-adhd/features/child-adhd-parental-relationship

7   THANKS

In this book, I have included all the knowledge, strategies and solutions I have learned in these 20 years of work and continuos study.

I hope you have enjoyed this publication, which took me months of work and sacrifices.

Thank you for reading this book; I admit it was not easy to make this publication. I hope it will be useful to you, and I would be happy to receive your opinion with an unbiased and honest review; it would mean a lot to me and help me improve in future publications.

Thank you very much. I hope to update the book soon with lots of new tips. I will look forward to your best suggestions.

Jennifer Mind

Made in United States
Orlando, FL
26 March 2022

16161536R00114